The Resilient Child

Self-help, Volume 1

Timothy Scott Phillips

Published by Arcane Horizons Publishing, 2024.

THE RESILIENT CHILD

First edition. November 26, 2024.

ISBN: 979-8230638988

Written by Timothy Scott Phillips.

Table of Contents

To all the resilient souls who have faced the storm of parental addiction and refused to let it define their future.

This book is for the child within you who yearned for safety, the adult you've become who seeks healing, and the courageous person you are today who dares to hope.

May you find strength in your journey, peace in your heart, and the power to create a life filled with love, purpose, and joy.

You are proof that resilience can transform pain into possibility.

Chapter 1: Introduction to Parental Addiction

Understanding Substance Abuse

Substance abuse is a complex and multifaceted issue that affects millions of people worldwide. It encompasses the misuse of various substances, including alcohol, prescription medications, and illegal drugs. To understand the impact of parental addiction, it is crucial to first grasp what substance abuse entails, its causes, and its effects on individuals and their families.

Substance abuse often begins as a voluntary act, with individuals choosing to consume alcohol or drugs for recreational or medicinal purposes. However, over time, repeated use can lead to physical and psychological dependence. This transition from voluntary use to addiction involves changes in brain chemistry, which make it increasingly difficult for individuals to control their consumption despite adverse consequences.

Several factors contribute to the development of substance abuse. Genetic predisposition plays a significant role; individuals with a family history of addiction are more likely to develop similar problems. Environmental factors, such as exposure to drugs at an early age, peer pressure, and stressful life events, also contribute to the risk. Psychological factors, including mental health disorders like depression, anxiety, and trauma, can further exacerbate the likelihood of substance abuse.

Substance abuse can have devastating effects on an individual's health, relationships, and overall well-being. Physically, it can lead to a range of health problems, including liver disease, cardiovascular issues, respiratory problems, and weakened immune systems. Psychologically, addiction often coexists with mental health disorders, creating a vicious cycle that is difficult to break. Socially, substance abuse can strain relationships, lead to job loss, financial instability, and legal issues.

Impact of Addiction on Family Dynamics

THE EFFECTS OF ADDICTION extend beyond the individual, profoundly impacting family dynamics and relationships. When a parent struggles with substance abuse, the entire family system is disrupted. The home, which should be a safe and nurturing environment, becomes a place of unpredictability, fear, and instability.

One of the most significant impacts of parental addiction is the erosion of trust. Children rely on their parents for stability, guidance, and support. When a parent is addicted, they are often unable to fulfill these roles consistently. Promises are broken, behaviors are erratic, and children learn that they cannot depend on their addicted parent. This loss of trust can have long-lasting effects on children's ability to form healthy relationships in the future.

Communication within the family often breaks down as well. Addiction is frequently accompanied by secrecy, denial, and dishonesty. Parents may lie about their substance use, hide their addiction, or minimize its severity. Children, in turn, may become secretive about their feelings, fears, and experiences, fearing judgment or repercussions. This lack of open communication creates an environment where issues are not addressed, and emotional needs are unmet.

Roles within the family can also become distorted. In many cases, children of substance-abusing parents take on adult responsibilities prematurely. They may become caregivers for their siblings or even their addicted parent, sacrificing their own needs and childhood experiences. This phenomenon, known as "parentification," places an enormous burden on children and can hinder their emotional and psychological development.

Financial instability is another common consequence of parental addiction. Substance abuse can lead to job loss, legal issues, and excessive spending on drugs or alcohol. As a result, families may face financial hardships, including unpaid bills, lack of necessities, and even homelessness. The stress of financial instability further exacerbates the emotional and psychological toll on children.

The presence of addiction in the home can also expose children to risky behaviors and environments. Children may witness or experience domestic violence, neglect, and abuse. They may be exposed to criminal activities, such as drug dealing or theft, as parents engage in illegal behavior to support their addiction. These traumatic experiences can leave lasting scars and increase the likelihood of children developing their own substance abuse problems or mental health disorders.

Overview of Challenges Faced by Adult Children of Substance Abusers

GROWING UP IN A HOUSEHOLD affected by parental addiction presents numerous challenges that can extend well into adulthood. Adult children of substance abusers often carry the emotional, psychological, and behavioral scars from their childhood experiences, impacting various aspects of their lives.

Emotional Challenges:

1. TRUST ISSUES: AS previously mentioned, trust is often severely damaged in families affected by addiction. Adult children may struggle to trust others, fearing betrayal or abandonment. This can hinder their ability to form and maintain healthy relationships, both personally and professionally.

2. Self-Esteem and Self-Worth: Children of substance abusers may internalize the belief that they are unworthy of love and attention. This low self-esteem can persist into adulthood, affecting their confidence and ability to pursue their goals and aspirations.

3. Guilt and Shame: Many adult children feel a deep sense of guilt and shame related to their parent's addiction. They may blame themselves for their parent's behavior or feel responsible for their parent's well-being. This misplaced guilt can lead to chronic feelings of inadequacy and self-blame.

4. Emotional Regulation: Growing up in a chaotic and unpredictable environment can make it difficult for adult children to manage their emotions

effectively. They may struggle with anger, anxiety, depression, and other emotional difficulties, often resorting to unhealthy coping mechanisms to numb their pain.

Psychological Challenges:

1. MENTAL HEALTH DISORDERS: Adult children of substance abusers are at an increased risk of developing mental health disorders, including depression, anxiety, post-traumatic stress disorder (PTSD), and substance use disorders. The trauma and stress of their childhood experiences can have lasting effects on their mental well-being.

2. Attachment Issues: The instability and inconsistency of their parent's behavior can lead to attachment issues. Adult children may have difficulty forming secure attachments in their relationships, fearing intimacy and vulnerability.

3. Codependency: Many adult children develop codependent tendencies, where their self-worth and identity are tied to taking care of others. They may struggle to set boundaries, prioritize their needs, and maintain healthy relationships.

Behavioral Challenges:

1. RISKY BEHAVIORS: Growing up in an environment where substance abuse is normalized can increase the likelihood of adult children engaging in risky behaviors themselves. They may turn to alcohol or drugs as a means of coping with their pain and stress.

2. Perfectionism: In an attempt to gain control and approval, some adult children adopt perfectionistic tendencies. They may strive for excellence in all areas of their life, driven by a fear of failure and a need to prove their worth.

3. Avoidance: To protect themselves from further pain, adult children may develop avoidance behaviors. They may avoid conflict, difficult emotions, or situations that remind them of their past trauma.

Interpersonal Challenges:

1. RELATIONSHIP DIFFICULTIES: Trust issues, attachment problems, and emotional regulation difficulties can make it challenging for adult children to form and maintain healthy relationships. They may struggle with intimacy, fear rejection, and find it hard to express their needs and emotions.

2. Parenting Challenges: For those who become parents themselves, the cycle of addiction and dysfunctional family dynamics can be challenging to break. They may struggle with parenting skills, emotional availability, and creating a stable environment for their children.

Despite these challenges, it is important to recognize that adult children of substance abusers also possess remarkable resilience and strength. Many have developed coping skills and strategies that have enabled them to navigate their difficult circumstances and achieve personal growth and success.

Resilience and Coping Strategies:

1. SEEKING PROFESSIONAL Help: Many adult children benefit from therapy and counseling to address their emotional and psychological challenges. Therapy provides a safe space to process their experiences, develop healthy coping mechanisms, and work through unresolved trauma.

2. Building a Support Network: Surrounding themselves with supportive and understanding individuals is crucial for adult children. Friends, partners, and support groups can provide validation, empathy, and encouragement.

3. Self-Care and Mindfulness: Engaging in self-care practices and mindfulness techniques can help adult children manage their stress, regulate their emotions, and prioritize their well-being. Activities such as meditation, journaling, exercise, and creative expression can be particularly beneficial.

4. Setting Boundaries: Learning to set and maintain healthy boundaries is essential for adult children. This includes recognizing their limits, saying no when necessary, and protecting themselves from toxic or harmful relationships.

5. Education and Awareness: Educating themselves about addiction, its effects, and the dynamics of dysfunctional families can empower adult children to understand their experiences and make informed choices about their future.

Moving Forward:

WHILE THE CHALLENGES faced by adult children of substance abusers are significant, it is important to remember that healing and growth are possible. With the right support, resources, and strategies, adult children can overcome their past trauma, build healthy relationships, and create fulfilling lives.

This book aims to provide a comprehensive guide for adult children of substance abusers, offering insights, strategies, and encouragement for their journey toward resilience and empowerment. Each chapter will delve deeper into specific aspects of their experiences, providing practical tools and inspiring stories to support their healing and personal growth.

As we embark on this journey together, remember that you are not alone. Many have walked this path before you and have found strength and hope along the way. By acknowledging your past, embracing your resilience, and taking steps toward healing, you can create a brighter and more fulfilling future.

Chapter 2: The Emotional Roller Coaster

Common Emotional Struggles

Growing up in a household affected by parental addiction exposes children to a myriad of emotional challenges. These emotional struggles are often profound and complex, stemming from the instability and trauma experienced during their formative years. Understanding these common emotional struggles is the first step toward addressing and healing from them.

1. Anger: Anger is a prevalent emotion among adult children of substance abusers. This anger can be directed towards the addicted parent, the non-addicted parent, siblings, or even themselves. Anger often arises from feelings of betrayal, abandonment, and frustration. The unpredictability and chaos caused by a parent's addiction can lead to intense resentment and rage.

2. Guilt: Many adult children experience overwhelming guilt. They may feel guilty for their parent's addiction, believing that they somehow caused or contributed to it. This guilt can be exacerbated if they were unable to help or change their parent's behavior. Guilt can also stem from feelings of relief or happiness when they distance themselves from their addicted parent.

3. Shame: Shame is another common emotional struggle. Adult children often feel a deep sense of shame about their family situation. They may believe that their parent's addiction is a reflection of their own worth or character. This shame can lead to secrecy and isolation, as they may avoid sharing their experiences with others for fear of judgment.

4. Anxiety: Growing up in an unpredictable environment can lead to chronic anxiety. The constant worry about their parent's behavior, safety, and well-being can create a state of hyper-vigilance. This anxiety can persist into adulthood, making it difficult to relax and feel secure in relationships and situations.

5. Depression: The emotional burden of living with an addicted parent can contribute to feelings of sadness and hopelessness. Adult children may struggle with depression, feeling overwhelmed by the weight of their experiences. This depression can be compounded by feelings of isolation and a lack of support.

6. Fear: Fear is a pervasive emotion in households affected by addiction. Children may fear for their own safety, as well as the safety of their siblings and other family members. They may also fear the future, uncertain about what will happen if their parent's addiction continues or worsens.

7. Confusion: The conflicting messages and behaviors exhibited by an addicted parent can lead to confusion. Children may struggle to understand why their parent behaves the way they do, why they can't stop using substances, and why their family life is so chaotic. This confusion can create a sense of disorientation and helplessness.

8. Loneliness: Growing up with an addicted parent can be an isolating experience. Children may feel different from their peers, unable to relate to their experiences or share their own. This loneliness can persist into adulthood, making it difficult to form meaningful connections and feel a sense of belonging.

9. Grief: Grief is a common, yet often unacknowledged, emotion among adult children of substance abusers. They may grieve the loss of the parent they wish they had, the family life they never experienced, and the childhood they missed out on. This grief can be compounded by the ongoing nature of their parent's addiction, creating a sense of unresolved loss.

10. Hopelessness: The chronic stress and trauma of living with an addicted parent can lead to feelings of hopelessness. Adult children may struggle to see a way out of their situation, feeling trapped by their past and uncertain about their future. This hopelessness can impact their motivation and ability to pursue their goals and aspirations.

Identifying and Processing Feelings of Anger, Guilt, and Shame

ADDRESSING THE EMOTIONAL struggles associated with parental addiction requires a deep understanding of these emotions and a commitment to processing them in healthy ways. Identifying and processing feelings of anger, guilt, and shame is essential for healing and moving forward.

Identifying Anger:

1. RECOGNIZE THE TRIGGERS: Pay attention to situations, people, or memories that trigger feelings of anger. This can help you understand the underlying causes of your anger and identify patterns in your emotional responses.

2. Acknowledge the Anger: Allow yourself to acknowledge and accept your anger without judgment. It's important to validate your feelings and understand that anger is a natural and legitimate response to your experiences.

3. Journal Your Emotions: Writing down your thoughts and feelings can help you gain clarity and perspective on your anger. Journaling allows you to express your emotions in a safe and constructive way.

Processing Anger:

1. EXPRESS YOUR ANGER Healthily: Find healthy outlets for your anger, such as physical exercise, creative expression, or talking to a trusted friend or therapist. Avoid unhealthy coping mechanisms like substance abuse, self-harm, or aggression.

2. Practice Relaxation Techniques: Techniques like deep breathing, meditation, and progressive muscle relaxation can help you calm your mind and body when you feel anger rising. These practices can also reduce the overall intensity of your anger.

3. Seek Professional Help: If your anger feels overwhelming or uncontrollable, consider seeking the help of a therapist. Therapy can provide a safe space to explore and process your anger, and develop effective coping strategies.

Identifying Guilt:

1. DIFFERENTIATE BETWEEN Healthy and Unhealthy Guilt: Healthy guilt arises when you recognize that you have done something wrong and need to make amends. Unhealthy guilt, however, involves taking on responsibility for things that are beyond your control, such as your parent's addiction.

2. Examine the Origins: Reflect on where your guilt is coming from. Are you feeling guilty for things that happened in the past, or for things you believe you should have done differently? Understanding the origins of your guilt can help you address it more effectively.

3. Challenge Negative Beliefs: Identify and challenge the negative beliefs that contribute to your guilt. For example, if you believe that you are responsible for your parent's addiction, remind yourself that addiction is a complex issue with multiple contributing factors.

Processing Guilt:

1. FORGIVE YOURSELF: Practice self-forgiveness by acknowledging that you did the best you could with the resources and knowledge you had at the time. Recognize that you are not responsible for your parent's choices and actions.

2. Seek Support: Talk to a trusted friend, family member, or therapist about your feelings of guilt. Sharing your experiences with someone who understands and validates your emotions can help you feel less alone and more supported.

3. Focus on Positive Actions: Redirect your energy toward positive actions that align with your values and goals. This can include volunteering, helping others, or pursuing personal growth. Engaging in meaningful activities can help you feel more empowered and less burdened by guilt.

Identifying Shame:

1. UNDERSTAND THE DIFFERENCE Between Guilt and Shame: Guilt involves feeling bad about something you have done, while shame involves feeling bad about who you are. Recognizing this distinction can help you address shame more effectively.

2. Identify Shame Triggers: Pay attention to situations, people, or thoughts that trigger feelings of shame. Understanding these triggers can help you anticipate and manage your emotional responses.

3. Acknowledge and Validate Your Feelings: Allow yourself to acknowledge and validate your feelings of shame without judgment. Recognize that shame is a natural response to your experiences and that you have the right to feel what you feel.

Processing Shame:

1. CHALLENGE NEGATIVE Self-Perceptions: Identify and challenge the negative self-perceptions that contribute to your shame. Replace them with more realistic and compassionate beliefs about yourself.

2. Practice Self-Compassion: Treat yourself with the same kindness and understanding that you would offer to a friend. Practice self-compassion by recognizing your strengths, acknowledging your efforts, and accepting your imperfections.

3. Seek Connection: Shame thrives in isolation. Seek connection with others who can offer empathy, understanding, and support. Sharing your experiences with trusted individuals can help you feel less alone and more validated.

Strategies for Emotional Regulation

EMOTIONAL REGULATION involves the ability to manage and respond to your emotions in healthy and constructive ways. Developing effective emotional regulation skills is essential for navigating the emotional roller coaster associated with parental addiction.

1. Mindfulness and Meditation:

MINDFULNESS AND MEDITATION practices can help you become more aware of your thoughts and emotions, and cultivate a sense of calm and balance. Regular mindfulness practice can improve your ability to manage stress, reduce emotional reactivity, and enhance your overall well-being.

2. Deep Breathing Exercises:

DEEP BREATHING EXERCISES can help activate the body's relaxation response, reducing feelings of anxiety and stress. Techniques such as diaphragmatic breathing, 4-7-8 breathing, and box breathing can be particularly effective for calming the mind and body.

3. Progressive Muscle Relaxation:

PROGRESSIVE MUSCLE relaxation involves tensing and then relaxing different muscle groups in the body. This practice can help release physical tension and promote a sense of relaxation and calm. It can be particularly helpful for managing physical symptoms of stress and anxiety.

4. Journaling:

Journaling is a powerful tool for processing emotions and gaining clarity and perspective. Writing down your thoughts and feelings can help you understand and organize your emotions, identify patterns, and develop insights into your experiences.

5. Physical Activity:

REGULAR PHYSICAL ACTIVITY can have a positive impact on your emotional well-being. Exercise releases endorphins, which are natural mood enhancers, and can help reduce feelings of stress, anxiety, and depression. Find activities that you enjoy, such as walking, running, dancing, or yoga.

6. Creative Expression:

ENGAGING IN CREATIVE activities, such as painting, drawing, writing, or playing music, can provide a healthy outlet for your emotions. Creative expression allows you to explore and express your feelings in a non-verbal way, which can be particularly helpful when words are insufficient.

7. Seeking Social Support:

CONNECTING WITH OTHERS who understand and validate your experiences can provide emotional support and reduce feelings of isolation. Join support groups, connect with friends and family, or seek the guidance of a therapist to build a strong support network.

8. Setting Boundaries:

SETTING AND MAINTAINING healthy boundaries is essential for protecting your emotional well-being. Learn to recognize your limits and communicate them clearly to others. Practice saying no when necessary and prioritize your own needs and well-being.

9. Practicing Self-Compassion:

TREAT YOURSELF WITH kindness and understanding, especially during difficult times. Practice self-compassion by acknowledging your efforts, recognizing your strengths, and accepting your imperfections. Remind yourself that you are worthy of love and care.

10. Developing Healthy Coping Mechanisms:

IDENTIFY AND DEVELOP healthy coping mechanisms to manage stress and emotions. This can include activities such as reading, spending time in nature, practicing yoga, or engaging in hobbies that bring you joy and relaxation.

11. Seeking Professional Help:

IF YOU FIND IT CHALLENGING to manage your emotions on your own, consider seeking the help of a therapist or counselor. Professional support can provide valuable insights, strategies, and guidance for navigating your emotional struggles and promoting healing and growth.

12. Building Resilience:

BUILDING RESILIENCE involves developing the ability to bounce back from adversity and cope with challenges in a healthy way. Focus on cultivating a positive mindset, practicing gratitude, and developing problem-solving skills. Building resilience can help you navigate the ups and downs of life with greater strength and confidence.

Conclusion:

The emotional roller coaster experienced by adult children of substance abusers is a challenging and often overwhelming journey. However, by understanding and addressing the common emotional struggles, identifying and processing feelings of anger, guilt, and shame, and developing effective strategies for emotional regulation, it is possible to navigate this journey with resilience and strength.

Remember that healing is a process, and it takes time and effort. Be patient and compassionate with yourself as you work through your emotions and experiences. Seek support when needed, and prioritize your well-being and self-care. By taking these steps, you can create a brighter and more fulfilling future, free from the shadows of your past.

As you continue reading this book, you will find additional insights, strategies, and encouragement to support your healing journey. Each chapter will provide practical tools and inspiring stories to help you navigate the complexities of your experiences and move toward a life of resilience and empowerment.

Chapter 3: Coping Mechanisms: Healthy vs. Unhealthy

Recognizing Harmful Coping Strategies

Coping mechanisms are behaviors and strategies individuals use to manage stress, emotions, and difficult situations. For adult children of substance abusers, coping mechanisms are crucial for navigating the complex and often tumultuous environments they grow up in. However, not all coping mechanisms are beneficial; many can be harmful and counterproductive.

1. Substance Abuse:

ONE OF THE MOST COMMON harmful coping mechanisms is turning to substances like alcohol or drugs. This can create a vicious cycle, as children of substance abusers may replicate their parent's behavior in an attempt to escape their own pain and stress. While substances may provide temporary relief, they ultimately exacerbate emotional and psychological issues and can lead to addiction.

2. Self-Harm:

SOME INDIVIDUALS RESORT to self-harm as a way to cope with overwhelming emotions. This behavior, which includes cutting, burning, or other forms of self-injury, is a physical manifestation of inner turmoil. It provides a temporary distraction or release from emotional pain but can lead to serious physical and psychological harm.

3. Eating Disorders:

EATING DISORDERS, SUCH as anorexia, bulimia, and binge eating, can be another harmful coping strategy. These disorders often stem from a desire for control in an otherwise chaotic life. However, they lead to severe health problems and further psychological distress.

4. Aggression and Violence:

SOME INDIVIDUALS EXPRESS their inner pain and frustration through aggression or violence. This can manifest as verbal abuse, physical fights, or destructive behavior. Such actions harm relationships, perpetuate cycles of violence, and do not address the underlying issues causing the anger.

5. Avoidance and Denial:

AVOIDANCE AND DENIAL are passive coping strategies where individuals refuse to acknowledge or confront their problems. This can involve ignoring emotional pain, avoiding difficult conversations, or procrastinating on important tasks. While these strategies might provide short-term relief, they prevent individuals from addressing and resolving their issues.

6. Overworking:

Overworking or becoming a workaholic is another harmful coping mechanism. By immersing themselves in work, individuals can distract themselves from personal issues and emotional pain. However, this can lead to burnout, stress-related health problems, and neglect of personal relationships and self-care.

7. Perfectionism:

Perfectionism is the relentless pursuit of flawlessness. While striving for excellence can be positive, perfectionism often leads to unrealistic expectations, chronic dissatisfaction, and intense self-criticism. It can be a way to cope with feelings of inadequacy but ultimately causes more harm than good.

8. Isolation:

Withdrawing from social interactions and isolating oneself is a common coping strategy. This can be due to feelings of shame, fear of judgment, or the desire to avoid further pain. However, isolation exacerbates loneliness and deprives individuals of the support and connection needed for healing.

9. Compulsive Behaviors:

COMPULSIVE BEHAVIORS, such as excessive gambling, shopping, or internet use, can serve as distractions from emotional pain. While these behaviors might provide temporary relief, they can lead to addiction, financial problems, and further emotional distress.

10. Blaming Others:

SHIFTING BLAME ONTO others is a defense mechanism that helps individuals avoid taking responsibility for their actions and emotions. While this may protect one's ego temporarily, it prevents personal growth and damages relationships.

Recognizing these harmful coping strategies is the first step toward change. It's essential to understand that while these behaviors may have provided temporary relief in the past, they ultimately hinder emotional and psychological well-being. Transitioning from harmful to healthy coping mechanisms requires self-awareness, commitment, and often, professional support.

Developing and Practicing Healthy Coping Skills

HEALTHY COPING SKILLS are behaviors and strategies that promote emotional and psychological well-being, helping individuals manage stress and navigate life's challenges effectively. Developing and practicing these skills can significantly enhance the quality of life for adult children of substance abusers.

1. Mindfulness and Meditation:

MINDFULNESS INVOLVES paying attention to the present moment without judgment. It helps individuals become aware of their thoughts and emotions, reducing stress and increasing emotional regulation. Meditation, a practice of focused attention and relaxation, can enhance mindfulness. Regular practice of mindfulness and meditation can lead to improved mental clarity, reduced anxiety, and greater emotional resilience.

2. Physical Exercise:

REGULAR PHYSICAL ACTIVITY is a powerful tool for managing stress and improving overall well-being. Exercise releases endorphins, which are natural mood enhancers. It also helps reduce anxiety, improve sleep, and boost self-esteem. Incorporating activities like walking, running, yoga, or dancing into daily routines can have significant positive effects on emotional and physical health.

3. Journaling:

Journaling is a therapeutic way to process thoughts and emotions. Writing about experiences, feelings, and challenges can provide clarity and insight. It allows individuals to express themselves freely and reflect on their growth. Journaling can also help identify patterns in thoughts and behaviors, aiding in the development of healthier coping strategies.

4. Seeking Social Support:

BUILDING A STRONG SUPPORT network is crucial for emotional well-being. Friends, family members, and support groups can provide empathy, understanding, and encouragement. Sharing experiences with others who have faced similar challenges can reduce feelings of isolation and provide valuable perspectives.

5. Setting Boundaries:

LEARNING TO SET AND maintain healthy boundaries is essential for protecting emotional well-being. This involves recognizing personal limits and communicating them clearly to others. Boundaries help prevent burnout, reduce stress, and promote healthier relationships. It's important to practice assertiveness and self-respect in setting boundaries.

6. Engaging in Creative Activities:

CREATIVE EXPRESSION, such as painting, drawing, writing, or playing music, provides a healthy outlet for emotions. These activities can be therapeutic, offering a way to process feelings and experiences non-verbally. Engaging in creative pursuits can also enhance self-esteem and provide a sense of accomplishment.

7. Practicing Gratitude:

GRATITUDE PRACTICES, such as keeping a gratitude journal or regularly reflecting on things to be thankful for, can shift focus from negative to positive aspects of life. Practicing gratitude has been shown to improve mood, increase resilience, and enhance overall well-being. It encourages a positive mindset and helps individuals appreciate the good in their lives.

8. Developing Problem-Solving Skills:

EFFECTIVE PROBLEM-SOLVING skills help individuals navigate challenges and make informed decisions. This involves identifying the problem, brainstorming possible solutions, evaluating the pros and cons of each option, and implementing the best solution. Developing these skills can reduce feelings of helplessness and increase confidence in managing difficult situations.

9. Seeking Professional Help:

THERAPY AND COUNSELING provide valuable support for addressing emotional and psychological challenges. A trained therapist can help individuals explore their experiences, develop healthy coping strategies, and work through unresolved trauma. Professional help can provide insights, tools, and a safe space for healing and growth.

10. Practicing Self-Compassion:

SELF-COMPASSION INVOLVES treating oneself with kindness, understanding, and forgiveness. It means recognizing that everyone makes mistakes and experiences difficulties. Practicing self-compassion can reduce self-criticism, enhance emotional resilience, and promote overall well-being. It encourages a more nurturing and supportive relationship with oneself.

11. Engaging in Relaxation Techniques:

RELAXATION TECHNIQUES, such as deep breathing, progressive muscle relaxation, and guided imagery, can help reduce stress and promote a sense of calm. These techniques activate the body's relaxation response, counteracting the effects of stress and anxiety. Regular practice of relaxation techniques can improve emotional regulation and overall well-being.

12. Building Healthy Routines:

ESTABLISHING AND MAINTAINING healthy routines can provide structure and stability. This includes regular sleep patterns, balanced nutrition, and consistent exercise. Healthy routines help manage stress, improve physical health, and enhance overall well-being. They provide a foundation for positive habits and behaviors.

13. Engaging in Community Activities:

INVOLVEMENT IN COMMUNITY activities, such as volunteering, joining clubs, or participating in local events, can provide a sense of purpose and connection. Engaging with the community fosters social interaction, builds relationships, and promotes a sense of belonging. It can also provide opportunities for personal growth and development.

14. Practicing Positive Self-Talk:

POSITIVE SELF-TALK involves replacing negative and self-critical thoughts with encouraging and supportive ones. This practice can improve self-esteem, reduce stress, and enhance overall well-being. Positive self-talk helps shift focus from limitations to strengths and possibilities, promoting a more optimistic outlook on life.

15. Developing a Growth Mindset:

A GROWTH MINDSET INVOLVES believing in the potential for growth and change. It encourages viewing challenges as opportunities for learning and development. Embracing a growth mindset can increase resilience, enhance motivation, and promote a positive approach to life's difficulties. It fosters a sense of empowerment and self-efficacy.

By developing and practicing these healthy coping skills, individuals can enhance their emotional and psychological well-being, build resilience, and navigate life's challenges more effectively. Transitioning from harmful to healthy coping mechanisms requires commitment and perseverance, but the rewards are well worth the effort.

Building Resilience Through Positive Habits

RESILIENCE IS THE ABILITY to adapt and thrive in the face of adversity. For adult children of substance abusers, building resilience is crucial for overcoming the challenges and trauma of their past. Positive habits and practices play a significant role in developing and sustaining resilience.

1. Establishing a Routine:

HAVING A STRUCTURED routine provides a sense of stability and predictability. It helps individuals manage their time effectively, reduce stress, and maintain a balanced lifestyle. A routine that includes healthy habits such as regular exercise, adequate sleep, and nutritious meals supports physical and emotional well-being.

2. Setting Realistic Goals:

SETTING REALISTIC AND achievable goals provides direction and motivation. It helps individuals focus on their strengths and build a sense of accomplishment. Breaking larger goals into smaller, manageable steps can make them more attainable and less overwhelming. Celebrating progress and milestones along the way reinforces a positive mindset.

3. Practicing Self-Care:

SELF-CARE INVOLVES taking intentional actions to care for one's physical, emotional, and mental health. This includes activities that bring joy, relaxation, and rejuvenation. Regular self-care practices, such as reading, taking baths, spending time in nature, or engaging in hobbies, promote overall well-being and resilience.

4. Cultivating Positive Relationships:

BUILDING AND MAINTAINING positive relationships is essential for emotional support and resilience. Surrounding oneself with supportive, understanding, and encouraging individuals fosters a sense of connection and belonging. Positive relationships provide a buffer against stress and enhance overall well-being.

5. Practicing Gratitude:

GRATITUDE PRACTICES help shift focus from negative experiences to positive aspects of life. Regularly reflecting on things to be thankful for promotes a positive mindset and enhances emotional resilience. Gratitude can be practiced through journaling, expressing appreciation to others, or simply taking time to reflect on positive moments.

6. Engaging in Lifelong Learning:

LIFELONG LEARNING INVOLVES seeking new knowledge, skills, and experiences. It fosters personal growth, adaptability, and a sense of purpose. Engaging in educational activities, attending workshops, or exploring new hobbies promotes cognitive and emotional resilience. It encourages a proactive approach to life's challenges.

7. Embracing Flexibility:

RESILIENCE INVOLVES being adaptable and open to change. Embracing flexibility means being willing to adjust plans, perspectives, and behaviors in response to new information and circumstances. It involves viewing challenges as opportunities for growth and learning. Flexibility enhances problem-solving skills and reduces stress.

8. Practicing Mindfulness:

MINDFULNESS INVOLVES being present in the moment and fully engaging with one's thoughts and emotions without judgment. Regular mindfulness practice reduces stress, improves emotional regulation, and enhances overall well-being. Mindfulness can be practiced through meditation, deep breathing, or simply paying attention to daily activities.

9. Fostering Optimism:

OPTIMISM INVOLVES MAINTAINING a positive outlook and focusing on the potential for positive outcomes. It encourages a hopeful and proactive approach to life's challenges. Fostering optimism can be achieved through positive self-talk, setting realistic goals, and seeking out positive experiences and relationships.

10. Developing Problem-Solving Skills:

EFFECTIVE PROBLEM-SOLVING skills are essential for navigating challenges and building resilience. This involves identifying problems, brainstorming solutions, evaluating options, and implementing the best course of action. Developing these skills enhances confidence and reduces feelings of helplessness.

11. Practicing Self-Compassion:

SELF-COMPASSION INVOLVES treating oneself with kindness and understanding, especially during difficult times. It means recognizing that everyone experiences challenges and setbacks. Practicing self-compassion reduces self-criticism, enhances emotional resilience, and promotes overall well-being.

12. Engaging in Relaxation Techniques:

REGULAR PRACTICE OF relaxation techniques, such as deep breathing, progressive muscle relaxation, and guided imagery, promotes a sense of calm and reduces stress. These techniques activate the body's relaxation response, counteracting the effects of stress and anxiety. They enhance emotional regulation and overall well-being.

13. Building a Support Network:

HAVING A STRONG SUPPORT network provides emotional and practical support during difficult times. Friends, family members, support groups, and therapists can offer empathy, understanding, and encouragement. Building and maintaining a support network fosters a sense of connection and resilience.

14. Practicing Patience:

BUILDING RESILIENCE is a gradual process that requires patience and persistence. Practicing patience involves recognizing that growth and healing take time. It means being kind to oneself and acknowledging progress, no matter how small. Patience fosters a positive mindset and encourages continued effort.

15. Fostering a Sense of Purpose:

HAVING A SENSE OF PURPOSE provides direction and motivation. It involves identifying meaningful goals and activities that align with one's values and passions. Fostering a sense of purpose enhances overall well-being, promotes resilience, and provides a sense of fulfillment.

By incorporating these positive habits into daily life, individuals can build and sustain resilience. Resilience is not an innate trait but a set of skills and behaviors that can be developed and strengthened over time. It involves a proactive approach to life's challenges, a positive mindset, and a commitment to self-care and personal growth.

Conclusion:

Navigating the complexities and emotional challenges of growing up with a substance-abusing parent requires effective coping mechanisms and resilience. Recognizing harmful coping strategies and transitioning to healthy ones is essential for emotional and psychological well-being. By developing and practicing healthy coping skills and building resilience through positive habits, individuals can overcome their past trauma, enhance their overall well-being, and create fulfilling lives.

Remember that building resilience and developing healthy coping mechanisms is a journey that requires commitment, patience, and support. Be kind and compassionate with yourself as you navigate this journey. Seek support when needed, prioritize self-care, and celebrate your progress and growth. By taking these steps, you can create a brighter and more resilient future.

As you continue reading this book, you will find additional insights, strategies, and encouragement to support your healing journey. Each chapter will provide practical tools and inspiring stories to help you navigate the complexities of your experiences and move toward a life of resilience and empowerment.

Chapter 4: The Legacy of Trust Issues

Trust and Relationships

Trust is the foundation of all healthy relationships. It is the belief that others will act with integrity, honesty, and reliability. For adult children of substance abusers, trust is often an elusive and fragile concept. Growing up in an environment where promises were frequently broken, behaviors were unpredictable, and deception was common, it is no surprise that trust issues become a significant challenge in their adult lives.

1. Trust and Its Importance:

TRUST IS ESSENTIAL for emotional safety and security in relationships. It allows individuals to be vulnerable, share their thoughts and feelings, and rely on others for support. Without trust, relationships become strained, and individuals may feel isolated, anxious, and disconnected. Trust builds the foundation for intimacy, cooperation, and mutual respect.

2. The Impact of Parental Addiction on Trust:

CHILDREN OF SUBSTANCE abusers often witness erratic and unreliable behavior from their addicted parent. Promises are made and broken, responsibilities are neglected, and trust is repeatedly violated. This inconsistency leads to a deep-seated fear of betrayal and abandonment. The non-addicted parent, if present, may also struggle with trust issues, either by enabling the addicted parent or failing to protect the children from harm. As a result, children learn that trust is dangerous and unreliable.

3. Trust Issues in Adult Relationships:

THE LEGACY OF BROKEN trust extends into adulthood, affecting relationships with friends, partners, colleagues, and even authority figures. Adult children of substance abusers may struggle to believe in the reliability and honesty of others, leading to difficulties in forming and maintaining healthy relationships. They may constantly doubt others' intentions, fear betrayal, and have difficulty opening up and being vulnerable.

4. Symptoms of Trust Issues:

- SUSPICION AND PARANOIA: Constantly questioning others' motives and actions.

- Fear of Vulnerability: Reluctance to share personal thoughts and feelings.

- Difficulty with Intimacy: Struggling to form close and meaningful connections.

- Avoidance of Commitment: Hesitancy to commit to relationships or long-term plans.

- Overcompensation: Trying to control relationships to prevent betrayal.

- Self-Sabotage: Ending relationships prematurely due to fear of eventual betrayal.

- Low Self-Esteem: Believing oneself to be unworthy of trust and love.

Understanding these symptoms is crucial for addressing and overcoming trust issues. Recognizing how past experiences shape current behavior is the first step toward healing and building healthier relationships.

Overcoming Betrayal and Mistrust

HEALING FROM BETRAYAL and mistrust requires a multifaceted approach that addresses the root causes, challenges negative beliefs, and fosters new, healthier patterns of thinking and behavior. Here are some steps to overcome betrayal and mistrust:

1. Acknowledging the Impact of Past Betrayal:

THE FIRST STEP IN OVERCOMING betrayal is acknowledging its impact. This involves recognizing the ways in which past betrayals have affected your ability to trust others. Reflect on specific incidents and their emotional aftermath. Understand that these experiences have shaped your current behaviors and beliefs about trust.

2. Processing Emotions:

BETRAYAL OFTEN LEADS to a range of intense emotions, including anger, sadness, hurt, and fear. It is important to process these emotions in a healthy way. This can involve journaling, talking to a trusted friend or therapist, or engaging in creative expression. Allow yourself to feel and express these emotions without judgment.

3. Challenging Negative Beliefs:

BETRAYAL CAN LEAD TO negative beliefs about oneself and others. For example, you may believe that you are unworthy of trust or that others are inherently untrustworthy. Challenge these beliefs by examining the evidence for and against them. Replace negative beliefs with more balanced and realistic ones. For example, recognize that while some people may betray trust, not everyone will.

4. Setting Realistic Expectations:

UNREALISTIC EXPECTATIONS can set the stage for disappointment and further mistrust. Understand that no one is perfect, and everyone makes mistakes. Set realistic expectations for yourself and others, recognizing that trust is a gradual process that requires time and effort.

5. Practicing Forgiveness:

FORGIVENESS IS A POWERFUL tool for healing from betrayal. This does not mean condoning harmful behavior but rather releasing the hold that anger and resentment have on you. Forgiveness allows you to move forward and focus on building healthy relationships. Practice self-forgiveness as well, recognizing that you did the best you could in difficult circumstances.

6. Rebuilding Trust Gradually:

REBUILDING TRUST IS a gradual process that involves taking small, manageable steps. Start by trusting others in low-risk situations and gradually increase the level of trust as you feel more comfortable. Communicate openly about your trust issues and let others know what you need to feel secure.

7. Practicing Self-Compassion:

SELF-COMPASSION INVOLVES treating yourself with kindness and understanding, especially when dealing with trust issues. Recognize that healing from betrayal takes time and that it is okay to feel vulnerable and uncertain. Practice self-care and prioritize your emotional well-being.

8. Seeking Professional Help:

A THERAPIST OR COUNSELOR can provide valuable support and guidance in overcoming betrayal and mistrust. They can help you explore the root causes of your trust issues, develop healthy coping strategies, and work through difficult emotions. Professional help can be especially beneficial if trust issues are deeply ingrained and affect multiple areas of your life.

9. Building a Support Network:

SURROUND YOURSELF WITH supportive and trustworthy individuals who understand your struggles and encourage your healing journey. A strong support network can provide validation, empathy, and encouragement. Engage with support groups, friends, family members, and mentors who can offer guidance and perspective.

10. Practicing Mindfulness:

MINDFULNESS INVOLVES being present in the moment and observing your thoughts and emotions without judgment. Practicing mindfulness can help you become more aware of your trust issues and how they affect your behavior. It can also reduce anxiety and promote emotional regulation.

11. Developing Healthy Boundaries:

HEALTHY BOUNDARIES are essential for protecting your emotional well-being and fostering trust. Clearly communicate your needs and limits to others and respect their boundaries as well. Boundaries create a sense of safety and predictability in relationships, reducing the risk of betrayal.

12. Embracing Vulnerability:

VULNERABILITY IS AN integral part of building trust. Allow yourself to be open and honest with others, even if it feels uncomfortable. Share your thoughts and feelings, express your needs, and be willing to take emotional risks. Embracing vulnerability fosters deeper connections and mutual trust.

Building Healthy Relationships and Boundaries

HEALTHY RELATIONSHIPS and boundaries are crucial for overcoming trust issues and creating a fulfilling and secure life. Here are some strategies for building healthy relationships and establishing boundaries:

1. Understanding the Importance of Healthy Relationships:

HEALTHY RELATIONSHIPS are based on mutual respect, trust, and effective communication. They provide emotional support, validation, and a sense of belonging. Understanding the characteristics of healthy relationships can help you identify and cultivate them in your life.

2. Characteristics of Healthy Relationships:

- MUTUAL RESPECT: BOTH individuals value and respect each other's thoughts, feelings, and boundaries.

- Trust: There is a foundation of trust and reliability, with both individuals acting with integrity and honesty.

- Open Communication: Effective communication involves active listening, empathy, and expressing thoughts and feelings openly.

- Support: Both individuals provide emotional support, encouragement, and validation to each other.

- Independence: Each person maintains their individuality and pursues their interests and goals.

- Equality: There is a sense of equality and fairness in the relationship, with both individuals contributing and receiving equally.

- Healthy Conflict Resolution: Conflicts are addressed constructively, with both individuals working toward resolution and understanding.

3. Building Healthy Relationships:

- BE AUTHENTIC: BE YOURSELF and allow others to see the real you. Authenticity fosters genuine connections and trust.

- Communicate Openly: Practice open and honest communication, expressing your thoughts, feelings, and needs. Listen actively and empathetically to others.

- Show Respect: Respect others' boundaries, opinions, and feelings. Treat others with kindness and consideration.

- Offer Support: Be supportive and encouraging, offering emotional and practical help when needed.

- Set Realistic Expectations: Set realistic and achievable expectations for yourself and others. Avoid placing unrealistic demands on relationships.

- Practice Forgiveness: Be willing to forgive and move forward from misunderstandings and mistakes. Hold space for growth and learning.

- Invest Time and Effort: Building and maintaining healthy relationships requires time and effort. Make an effort to nurture and strengthen your connections.

4. Establishing Healthy Boundaries:

BOUNDARIES ARE ESSENTIAL for protecting your emotional well-being and maintaining healthy relationships. They define what is acceptable and unacceptable behavior and help create a sense of safety and respect.

Steps to Establish Healthy Boundaries:

1. IDENTIFY YOUR NEEDS: Reflect on your needs, values, and limits. Understand what makes you feel safe, respected, and valued.

2. Communicate Clearly: Clearly communicate your boundaries to others. Be assertive and direct, using "I" statements to express your needs.

3. Be Consistent: Consistently enforce your boundaries and follow through with consequences if they are violated. Consistency reinforces the importance of your boundaries.

4. Respect Others' Boundaries: Respect and honor the boundaries of others. Recognize that boundaries are mutual and essential for healthy relationships.

5. Practice Self-Awareness: Stay aware of your feelings and reactions. If a boundary is crossed, address it promptly and assertively.

6. Seek Support: If you find it challenging to set or maintain boundaries, seek support from a therapist or counselor. They can provide guidance and strategies for boundary-setting.

Examples of Healthy Boundaries:

- EMOTIONAL BOUNDARIES: Expressing your feelings and needs, and not allowing others to manipulate or control your emotions.

- Physical Boundaries: Respecting personal space and physical touch preferences.

- Time Boundaries: Prioritizing your time and commitments, and not overcommitting to others.

- Intellectual Boundaries: Respecting differing opinions and beliefs, and not allowing others to belittle or dismiss your thoughts.

- Material Boundaries: Setting limits on sharing or lending personal belongings and finances.

5. Navigating Relationship Challenges:

EVEN IN HEALTHY RELATIONSHIPS, challenges and conflicts are inevitable. Navigating these challenges constructively is essential for maintaining trust and strengthening connections.

Strategies for Navigating Relationship Challenges:

- ADDRESS ISSUES PROMPTLY: Address conflicts and misunderstandings as they arise, rather than allowing them to fester. Prompt resolution prevents resentment and mistrust.

- Practice Active Listening: Listen actively and empathetically to the other person's perspective. Validate their feelings and show understanding.

- Express Yourself Clearly: Communicate your thoughts and feelings clearly and assertively. Avoid passive-aggressive behavior and be direct in your communication.

- Seek Compromise: Work toward mutually acceptable solutions that consider both parties' needs and perspectives. Compromise fosters cooperation and mutual respect.

- Take Responsibility: Take responsibility for your actions and behavior. Acknowledge mistakes and work toward making amends.

- Seek Mediation if Needed: If conflicts persist and cannot be resolved independently, consider seeking mediation or couples therapy. A neutral third party can provide guidance and facilitate resolution.

6. Building Trust in New Relationships:

BUILDING TRUST IN NEW relationships requires time, effort, and a commitment to authenticity and openness. Here are some steps to build trust:

Steps to Build Trust in New Relationships:

1. BE HONEST: PRACTICE honesty and transparency in your interactions. Avoid deception or hiding important information.

2. Show Consistency: Demonstrate consistency in your words and actions. Reliability fosters trust.

3. Communicate Openly: Share your thoughts, feelings, and experiences openly. Encourage open communication from the other person as well.

4. Respect Boundaries: Respect and honor the other person's boundaries and expect the same in return.

5. Be Patient: Trust takes time to develop. Be patient and allow the relationship to grow naturally.

6. Demonstrate Empathy: Show empathy and understanding toward the other person's experiences and feelings. Empathy fosters connection and trust.

7. Build Shared Experiences: Engage in activities and experiences together that foster connection and understanding.

7. Healing from Past Trust Issues:

HEALING FROM PAST TRUST issues involves a commitment to self-awareness, self-compassion, and personal growth. Here are some steps to facilitate healing:

Steps to Heal from Past Trust Issues:

1. REFLECT ON PAST Experiences: Reflect on past experiences that contributed to your trust issues. Understand how these experiences shaped your beliefs and behaviors.

2. Challenge Negative Beliefs: Identify and challenge negative beliefs about trust and relationships. Replace them with more balanced and realistic perspectives.

3. Practice Self-Compassion: Treat yourself with kindness and understanding. Recognize that healing takes time and effort.

4. Engage in Therapy: Consider seeking therapy to explore and address trust issues. A therapist can provide valuable support and guidance.

5. Build Positive Relationships: Surround yourself with supportive and trustworthy individuals who encourage your healing journey.

6. Set and Maintain Boundaries: Establish and enforce healthy boundaries to protect your emotional well-being.

7. Embrace Vulnerability: Allow yourself to be vulnerable and open in relationships. Embracing vulnerability fosters deeper connections and mutual trust.

8. Building Trust in Yourself:

BUILDING TRUST IN YOURSELF is essential for overcoming trust issues and creating a fulfilling life. Self-trust involves believing in your ability to make decisions, handle challenges, and navigate relationships.

Steps to Build Trust in Yourself:

1. ACKNOWLEDGE YOUR Strengths: Recognize and celebrate your strengths, accomplishments, and positive qualities.

2. Practice Self-Reflection: Engage in regular self-reflection to understand your thoughts, feelings, and behaviors.

3. Set Realistic Goals: Set and achieve realistic goals that align with your values and aspirations.

4. Take Responsibility: Take responsibility for your actions and decisions. Acknowledge and learn from mistakes.

5. Practice Self-Care: Prioritize self-care and well-being. Engage in activities that nurture your physical, emotional, and mental health.

6. Build Self-Confidence: Engage in activities that boost self-confidence, such as learning new skills or pursuing hobbies.

7. Trust Your Intuition: Trust your instincts and intuition. Listen to your inner voice and make decisions that align with your values and beliefs.

Conclusion:

The legacy of trust issues for adult children of substance abusers is a significant challenge that affects relationships, emotional well-being, and overall life satisfaction. However, by understanding the impact of trust issues, overcoming betrayal and mistrust, and building healthy relationships and boundaries, it is possible to heal and create a fulfilling and secure life.

Remember that healing from trust issues is a journey that requires self-awareness, self-compassion, and a commitment to personal growth. Be patient and kind to yourself as you navigate this journey. Seek support when needed, prioritize your well-being, and celebrate your progress and growth. By taking these steps, you can create a brighter and more resilient future.

As you continue reading this book, you will find additional insights, strategies, and encouragement to support your healing journey. Each chapter will provide practical tools and inspiring stories to help you navigate the complexities of your experiences and move toward a life of resilience and empowerment.

Chapter 5: Navigating Family Dynamics

Managing Relationships with the Addicted Parent

Managing relationships with an addicted parent can be incredibly challenging. The unpredictability, emotional turmoil, and often manipulative behavior associated with addiction create a complex environment for adult children. These relationships are typically marked by a mix of love, resentment, hope, and despair. Here are some strategies to navigate this complex dynamic effectively:

1. Understanding Addiction:

TO MANAGE A RELATIONSHIP with an addicted parent, it is crucial to understand the nature of addiction. Addiction is a chronic disease characterized by compulsive drug seeking and use despite harmful consequences. It affects brain function and behavior, making it difficult for the addicted person to control their substance use. Recognizing that addiction is a disease can foster empathy and reduce personal guilt or blame.

2. Setting Realistic Expectations:

SETTING REALISTIC EXPECTATIONS is essential. Understand that your parent may not be capable of providing the support or relationship you desire. Accepting their limitations can help prevent repeated disappointment and emotional pain. It's important to focus on what is within your control and not on changing the addicted parent.

3. Communicating Effectively:

EFFECTIVE COMMUNICATION involves being honest and clear about your feelings and needs while also listening to the addicted parent's perspective. Use "I" statements to express how their behavior affects you, such as "I feel hurt when you break promises." Avoid blaming or shaming language, which can escalate conflict and defensiveness.

4. Establishing Boundaries:

BOUNDARIES ARE CRUCIAL for protecting your emotional and physical well-being. Clearly define what behaviors you will and will not tolerate. For example, you might decide not to lend money to your addicted parent or to leave the situation if they become verbally abusive. Consistently enforce these boundaries to maintain your own stability.

5. Practicing Self-Care:

CARING FOR AN ADDICTED parent can be emotionally and physically draining. Prioritize your own self-care by engaging in activities that promote relaxation and well-being, such as exercise, meditation, hobbies, and spending time with supportive friends. Taking care of yourself ensures that you have the strength and resilience to navigate the relationship.

6. Seeking Support:

DON'T HESITATE TO SEEK support from therapists, support groups, or trusted friends. Sharing your experiences with others who understand can provide validation and practical advice. Support groups like Al-Anon can offer valuable resources and a sense of community.

7. Letting Go of Control:

IT'S IMPORTANT TO RECOGNIZE that you cannot control your parent's addiction or recovery. Letting go of the need to fix or save them can reduce stress and frustration. Focus on what you can control, such as your reactions and decisions, rather than trying to manage their behavior.

8. Encouraging Treatment:

WHILE YOU CANNOT FORCE your parent into treatment, you can express your concerns and encourage them to seek help. Provide information about treatment options and offer support in taking steps toward recovery. However, be prepared for resistance and understand that the decision to seek help must come from them.

9. Practicing Forgiveness:

FORGIVENESS IS A PERSONAL process that involves letting go of anger and resentment. This doesn't mean condoning harmful behavior, but rather freeing yourself from the burden of negative emotions. Forgiveness can be a powerful step toward healing and moving forward.

10. Planning for Safety:

IN SITUATIONS WHERE an addicted parent's behavior becomes dangerous, it's important to have a safety plan. This may involve seeking help from law enforcement, staying with friends or family, or accessing emergency resources. Your safety and well-being should always be the top priority.

Sibling Dynamics and Their Complexities

SIBLING RELATIONSHIPS in families affected by addiction can be particularly complex. Each sibling may respond differently to the chaos and stress, leading to varied coping mechanisms and relational dynamics. Understanding these complexities is essential for fostering healthy sibling relationships.

1. Differing Roles and Responsibilities:

IN FAMILIES WITH AN addicted parent, siblings often take on different roles and responsibilities. Some common roles include the caretaker, the enabler, the scapegoat, the lost child, and the hero. These roles can create tension and conflict among siblings as they navigate their unique experiences and coping mechanisms.

2. Communication and Support:

OPEN AND HONEST COMMUNICATION is key to navigating sibling dynamics. Encourage each other to share feelings, experiences, and concerns. Supporting one another can create a sense of unity and strength. Recognize that each sibling may have different needs and perspectives, and validate their experiences.

3. Addressing Resentment and Rivalry:

RESENTMENT AND RIVALRY can develop when siblings feel that responsibilities or attention are unequally distributed. Address these feelings by discussing them openly and finding ways to share responsibilities more equitably. Acknowledge and appreciate each other's efforts and contributions.

4. Seeking Mediation or Family Therapy:

IN CASES WHERE SIBLING dynamics become particularly strained, mediation or family therapy can be beneficial. A neutral third party can facilitate discussions, help resolve conflicts, and promote understanding. Therapy can also provide tools for improving communication and strengthening relationships.

5. Establishing Boundaries:

JUST AS WITH THE ADDICTED parent, establishing boundaries with siblings is important. Define what behaviors are acceptable and what you need to maintain your well-being. Respect each other's boundaries and work together to create a supportive and respectful environment.

6. Recognizing Individual Coping Mechanisms:

EACH SIBLING MAY DEVELOP different coping mechanisms in response to the family situation. Recognize and respect these differences, and avoid judging each other's coping strategies. Encourage healthy coping mechanisms and provide support in making positive changes.

7. Rebuilding Trust:

TRUST MAY BE DAMAGED among siblings due to the chaos and dysfunction caused by the addiction. Rebuilding trust involves being reliable, keeping promises, and being honest with each other. It's a gradual process that requires patience and consistency.

8. Navigating Differences in Perspectives:

SIBLINGS MAY HAVE DIFFERENT perspectives on the addicted parent and the family situation. Respect these differences and avoid trying to convince each other to adopt a specific viewpoint. Focus on finding common ground and supporting each other despite differing opinions.

9. Providing Mutual Support:

PROVIDE EMOTIONAL AND practical support to each other. This can involve listening, offering advice, helping with responsibilities, or simply being there for each other. Mutual support fosters a sense of solidarity and resilience.

10. Celebrating Positive Moments:

AMID THE CHALLENGES, find opportunities to celebrate positive moments and achievements together. Whether it's a personal milestone or a family event, these moments of joy can strengthen sibling bonds and create positive memories.

Setting and Maintaining Boundaries

SETTING AND MAINTAINING boundaries is crucial for navigating relationships with an addicted parent and siblings. Boundaries protect your emotional and physical well-being, promote healthy interactions, and prevent codependency. Here are steps to establish and enforce boundaries effectively:

1. Identifying Your Boundaries:

REFLECT ON YOUR NEEDS, values, and limits to identify what boundaries are necessary for your well-being. Consider what behaviors you find unacceptable, what situations cause you stress, and what you need to feel safe and respected.

2. Communicating Boundaries Clearly:

COMMUNICATE YOUR BOUNDARIES clearly and assertively. Use "I" statements to express your needs and limits, such as "I need to leave the room when there is yelling" or "I can't lend you money." Be direct and specific to avoid misunderstandings.

3. Consistently Enforcing Boundaries:

CONSISTENCY IS KEY to maintaining boundaries. Enforce your boundaries every time they are violated, and follow through with consequences if necessary. Consistency reinforces the importance of your boundaries and prevents others from testing them.

4. Handling Pushback and Resistance:

EXPECT SOME PUSHBACK or resistance when you set boundaries, especially if the other person is not used to them. Stand firm in your decisions and avoid getting drawn into arguments or justifications. Remain calm and assertive, reiterating your boundaries as needed.

5. Practicing Self-Respect:

RESPECTING YOUR OWN boundaries is essential for self-respect. Avoid compromising your boundaries to please others or avoid conflict. Recognize that setting boundaries is an act of self-care and self-respect, and prioritize your well-being.

6. Seeking Support:

SETTING AND MAINTAINING boundaries can be challenging, especially in dysfunctional family dynamics. Seek support from therapists, support groups, or trusted friends who can provide guidance and encouragement. They can offer valuable perspectives and help you stay committed to your boundaries.

7. Evaluating and Adjusting Boundaries:

BOUNDARIES MAY NEED to be adjusted over time as situations and relationships evolve. Regularly evaluate your boundaries to ensure they continue to meet your needs. Be flexible and willing to make changes if necessary, while still prioritizing your well-being.

8. Teaching and Modeling Boundaries:

IF YOU HAVE CHILDREN or younger siblings, teaching and modeling healthy boundaries is crucial. Demonstrate respect for your own and others' boundaries, and educate them on the importance of setting and maintaining their own boundaries. Encourage open communication and respect for personal limits.

9. Balancing Boundaries with Compassion:

WHILE SETTING BOUNDARIES is essential, it's also important to balance them with compassion and understanding. Recognize that the addicted parent or siblings may be struggling with their own challenges. Approach boundary-setting with empathy, while still prioritizing your well-being.

10. Celebrating Successes:

ACKNOWLEDGE AND CELEBRATE your successes in setting and maintaining boundaries. Recognize the positive impact on your well-being and relationships. Celebrating these successes reinforces your commitment to healthy boundaries and encourages continued growth.

Conclusion

Navigating family dynamics in the context of addiction is a complex and ongoing process. Managing relationships with an addicted parent, understanding and addressing sibling dynamics, and setting and maintaining boundaries are essential components of this journey. Each step requires self-awareness, patience, and a commitment to personal well-being.

Remember that you are not alone in this journey. Seek support from therapists, support groups, and trusted friends who understand your experiences.

Prioritize your self-care and well-being, and recognize that healing and growth take time. By implementing the strategies outlined in this chapter, you can navigate family dynamics more effectively, build healthier relationships, and create a more fulfilling and resilient life.

As you continue reading this book, you will find additional insights, strategies, and encouragement to support your healing journey. Each chapter provides practical tools and inspiring stories to help you navigate the complexities of your experiences and move toward a life of resilience and empowerment.

Chapter 6: Healing the Inner Child

Understanding the Concept of the Inner Child

The concept of the inner child is a crucial aspect of psychological healing and personal growth. The inner child represents the part of our psyche that retains the experiences, emotions, and memories from our childhood. This concept is not just metaphorical but also a psychological reality that influences our thoughts, feelings, and behaviors as adults.

1. Definition of the Inner Child:

THE INNER CHILD REFERS to a semi-independent subpersonality within our psyche that embodies the feelings, memories, and experiences of our younger self. It holds the innocence, creativity, and spontaneity of childhood but also the traumas, fears, and unmet needs from that time.

2. Origin and Development:

THE INNER CHILD DEVELOPS from our earliest experiences and interactions. Positive experiences and nurturing relationships contribute to a healthy and joyful inner child, while neglect, abuse, or trauma can create a wounded inner child. These early experiences shape our beliefs, self-esteem, and coping mechanisms.

3. Influence on Adult Behavior:

THE INNER CHILD INFLUENCES our adult behavior in significant ways. Unresolved childhood wounds can manifest as trust issues, low self-esteem, anxiety, depression, and dysfunctional relationship patterns. Conversely, nurturing and integrating the inner child can lead to greater emotional health, creativity, and joy.

4. Signs of a Wounded Inner Child:

COMMON SIGNS OF A WOUNDED inner child include:

- Difficulty trusting others and forming close relationships

- Persistent feelings of unworthiness or shame

- Emotional reactivity and difficulty regulating emotions

- A tendency to self-sabotage or engage in self-destructive behaviors

- Fear of abandonment and rejection

- A sense of being stuck in old patterns and unable to move forward

Understanding these signs is the first step in recognizing the need for inner child healing. Addressing these wounds requires patience, self-awareness, and a commitment to self-compassion.

Techniques for Nurturing and Healing Past Wounds

HEALING THE INNER CHILD involves acknowledging and addressing past wounds, providing the care and nurturing that may have been lacking during childhood. Here are several techniques to nurture and heal the inner child:

1. Inner Child Meditation:

MEDITATION IS A POWERFUL tool for connecting with and healing the inner child. Inner child meditation involves visualizing your younger self, offering comfort, and expressing love and understanding. This practice can help integrate past experiences and promote emotional healing.

Steps for Inner Child Meditation:

1. FIND A QUIET, COMFORTABLE space and close your eyes.

2. Take deep breaths to relax and center yourself.

3. Visualize your younger self at a specific age or during a significant memory.

4. Observe your inner child's emotions, appearance, and surroundings.

5. Approach your inner child with compassion and offer words of comfort and love.

6. Spend time with your inner child, engaging in activities they enjoy or simply being present.

7. Reassure your inner child that they are safe, loved, and valued.

8. Gradually bring your focus back to the present moment and reflect on the experience.

2. Journaling:

Journaling is an effective way to explore and process inner child wounds. Writing about past experiences, emotions, and memories can provide clarity and insight. It also allows for self-expression and emotional release.

Journaling Prompts for Inner Child Healing:

- DESCRIBE A HAPPY MEMORY from your childhood. How did it make you feel?

- Write a letter to your younger self, offering words of encouragement and love.

- Reflect on a difficult or traumatic childhood experience. How did it impact you?

- List the qualities you admire in your inner child. How can you nurture these qualities as an adult?

- Write about your inner child's needs and how you can meet them now.

3. Creative Expression:

ENGAGING IN CREATIVE activities such as drawing, painting, writing, or music can provide a healthy outlet for inner child healing. Creative expression allows you to reconnect with your playful, imaginative self and process emotions in a non-verbal way.

Activities for Creative Expression:

- DRAW OR PAINT A PICTURE that represents your inner child's feelings or experiences.

- Create a collage or vision board that reflects your inner child's dreams and aspirations.

- Write a story or poem from the perspective of your inner child.

- Play a musical instrument or create a song that expresses your inner child's emotions.

4. Therapy and Counseling:

WORKING WITH A THERAPIST or counselor can provide valuable support and guidance in healing the inner child. Therapeutic approaches such as inner child work, EMDR (Eye Movement Desensitization and Reprocessing), and trauma-focused therapy can help address past wounds and promote healing.

Benefits of Therapy for Inner Child Healing:

- A SAFE SPACE TO EXPLORE and process past experiences

- Professional guidance and support in addressing trauma and emotional wounds

- Development of healthy coping mechanisms and emotional regulation skills

- Greater self-awareness and understanding of how past experiences influence current behavior

5. Affirmations and Positive Self-Talk:

AFFIRMATIONS AND POSITIVE self-talk are powerful tools for nurturing the inner child. Repeating positive statements and reframing negative thoughts can help build self-esteem and promote a sense of worthiness and love.

Examples of Affirmations for Inner Child Healing:

- “I AM WORTHY OF LOVE and respect.”

- “I am safe and protected.”

- “I deserve happiness and joy.”

- “I forgive myself for past mistakes.”

- “I am proud of who I am and who I am becoming.”

6. Reparenting:

Reparenting involves providing the care, support, and nurturing that may have been lacking during childhood. This can include setting healthy boundaries, practicing self-care, and offering self-compassion and encouragement.

Steps for Reparenting:

1. IDENTIFY YOUR INNER child’s needs and unmet needs from childhood.

2. Develop a self-care routine that addresses these needs.

3. Set healthy boundaries to protect your emotional and physical well-being.

4. Offer yourself compassion and understanding, especially during difficult times.

5. Encourage and celebrate your achievements and progress.

7. Engaging in Play and Fun:

RECONNECTING WITH YOUR inner child involves embracing playfulness and fun. Engaging in activities that bring joy and laughter can help heal past wounds and foster a sense of freedom and creativity.

Activities for Embracing Play and Fun:

- SPEND TIME OUTDOORS, exploring nature and enjoying physical activities.

- Play games or engage in hobbies that you enjoyed as a child.

- Allow yourself to be spontaneous and try new experiences.

- Spend time with children or pets, embracing their playful energy.

8. Building Supportive Relationships:

SURROUNDING YOURSELF with supportive, nurturing relationships can provide a sense of safety and validation for your inner child. Seek out friendships and connections that offer empathy, understanding, and encouragement.

Steps to Build Supportive Relationships:

1. IDENTIFY INDIVIDUALS who are positive, supportive, and understanding.

2. Communicate openly and honestly with these individuals about your needs and experiences.

3. Engage in activities and spend quality time with supportive friends and family.

4. Set healthy boundaries to protect your well-being and foster mutual respect.

Exercises for Self-Compassion and Self-Love

SELF-COMPASSION AND self-love are essential components of healing the inner child. These practices involve treating yourself with kindness, understanding, and acceptance. Here are several exercises to cultivate self-compassion and self-love:

1. Loving-Kindness Meditation:

LOVING-KINDNESS MEDITATION involves sending feelings of love and compassion to yourself and others. This practice can help cultivate self-compassion and reduce negative self-judgment.

Steps for Loving-Kindness Meditation:

1. FIND A QUIET, COMFORTABLE space and close your eyes.

2. Take deep breaths to relax and center yourself.

3. Begin by focusing on yourself. Repeat the following phrases silently or aloud: "May I be happy. May I be healthy. May I be safe. May I live with ease."

4. Visualize sending these feelings of love and compassion to yourself.

5. Gradually expand your focus to include others, such as loved ones, friends, and even those with whom you have difficulties.

6. Continue to repeat the phrases, sending feelings of love and compassion to each person.

7. Conclude by bringing your focus back to yourself and reflecting on the experience.

2. Mirror Work:

MIRROR WORK INVOLVES looking at yourself in the mirror and speaking positive affirmations. This practice can help build self-love and improve self-esteem.

Steps for Mirror Work:

1. STAND IN FRONT OF a mirror and make eye contact with yourself.

2. Repeat positive affirmations, such as "I love you," "You are worthy," and "You are enough."

3. Focus on your reflection and observe any emotions or thoughts that arise.

4. Continue to repeat affirmations, offering yourself love and compassion.

5. Practice mirror work regularly to reinforce positive self-talk and self-love.

3. Self-Compassion Break:

A SELF-COMPASSION BREAK involves taking a moment to offer yourself kindness and understanding during difficult times. This practice can help reduce stress and promote emotional resilience.

Steps for a Self-Compassion Break:

1. WHEN YOU NOTICE yourself feeling stressed or overwhelmed, take a moment to pause.

2. Acknowledge your feelings and recognize that it's okay to feel this way.

3. Place your hand over your heart and take a few deep breaths.

4. Repeat the following phrases silently or aloud: "This is a moment of suffering. Suffering is a part of life. May I be kind to myself in this moment. May I give myself the compassion I need."

5. Reflect on the experience and allow yourself to feel the compassion and understanding.

4. Gratitude Practice:

PRACTICING GRATITUDE involves regularly reflecting on and appreciating the positive aspects of your life. This practice can help shift focus from negative to positive and foster a sense of self-love and contentment.

Steps for a Gratitude Practice:

1. SET ASIDE TIME EACH day to reflect on things you are grateful for.

2. Write down three to five things you appreciate about yourself and your life.

3. Reflect on these aspects and allow yourself to feel the gratitude and appreciation.

4. Consider expressing gratitude to others, whether through a note, a conversation, or an act of kindness.

5. Practice gratitude regularly to cultivate a positive mindset and self-love.

5. Self-Care Routine:

ESTABLISHING A SELF-care routine involves regularly engaging in activities that promote your physical, emotional, and mental well-being. This practice can help nurture your inner child and build self-love.

Steps for Establishing a Self-Care Routine:

1. IDENTIFY ACTIVITIES that bring you joy, relaxation, and rejuvenation.

2. Schedule regular time for these activities in your daily or weekly routine.

3. Prioritize self-care and treat it as an essential part of your well-being.

4. Be flexible and adjust your self-care routine as needed to meet your changing needs.

5. Reflect on the positive impact of self-care on your overall well-being and self-love.

6. Self-Compassion Journaling:

SELF-COMPASSION JOURNALING involves writing about your experiences, thoughts, and feelings with a focus on self-compassion and understanding. This practice can help you process emotions and cultivate self-love.

Self-Compassion Journaling Prompts:

- WRITE ABOUT A RECENT challenge or difficult experience. How did you handle it? How can you offer yourself compassion and understanding?

- Reflect on a time when you felt proud of yourself. What did you achieve, and how can you celebrate this accomplishment?

- Describe a quality or characteristic you appreciate about yourself. How can you nurture and embrace this quality?

- Write a letter to yourself, offering words of encouragement and love. What do you need to hear right now?

- Reflect on a moment when you felt loved and supported. How can you recreate this feeling for yourself?

7. Practicing Mindfulness:

MINDFULNESS INVOLVES being present in the moment and observing your thoughts and emotions without judgment. This practice can help you become more aware of your inner child's needs and foster self-compassion.

Steps for Practicing Mindfulness:

1. FIND A QUIET, COMFORTABLE space and close your eyes.

2. Take deep breaths to relax and center yourself.

3. Focus on the present moment, observing your thoughts, feelings, and sensations without judgment.

4. If your mind wanders, gently bring your focus back to the present moment.

5. Practice mindfulness regularly to enhance self-awareness and self-compassion.

8. Engaging in Positive Self-Talk:

POSITIVE SELF-TALK involves replacing negative and self-critical thoughts with encouraging and supportive ones. This practice can help build self-esteem and promote self-love.

Steps for Engaging in Positive Self-Talk:

1. NOTICE WHEN YOU have negative or self-critical thoughts.

2. Challenge these thoughts by examining the evidence for and against them.

3. Replace negative thoughts with positive and supportive statements.

4. Practice positive self-talk regularly to reinforce self-love and self-acceptance.

9. Creating a Self-Love Ritual:

A SELF-LOVE RITUAL involves engaging in activities that promote self-love and appreciation. This practice can help you connect with your inner child and nurture your well-being.

Steps for Creating a Self-Love Ritual:

1. CHOOSE ACTIVITIES that promote relaxation, joy, and self-care.

2. Set aside dedicated time for your self-love ritual, whether daily or weekly.

3. Engage in activities mindfully, focusing on the positive impact they have on your well-being.

4. Reflect on the experience and allow yourself to feel the love and appreciation.

5. Adjust your self-love ritual as needed to meet your changing needs and preferences.

10. Seeking Support and Connection:

BUILDING CONNECTIONS with others who understand and support your healing journey is essential for self-compassion and self-love. Seek out relationships that offer empathy, encouragement, and validation.

Steps for Seeking Support and Connection:

1. IDENTIFY INDIVIDUALS who are positive, supportive, and understanding.

2. Communicate openly and honestly with these individuals about your needs and experiences.

3. Engage in activities and spend quality time with supportive friends and family.

4. Join support groups or online communities that focus on inner child healing and self-compassion.

5. Build a network of supportive relationships that foster mutual respect and understanding.

Conclusion

Healing the inner child is a journey of self-discovery, compassion, and growth. Understanding the concept of the inner child, nurturing and healing past wounds, and practicing self-compassion and self-love are essential steps in this process. By implementing the techniques and exercises outlined in this chapter, you can reconnect with your inner child, heal past traumas, and create a fulfilling and joyful life.

Remember that healing takes time and effort. Be patient and compassionate with yourself as you navigate this journey. Seek support when needed, prioritize your well-being, and celebrate your progress and growth. By taking these steps, you can embrace your inner child and move toward a life of resilience, empowerment, and self-love.

As you continue reading this book, you will find additional insights, strategies, and encouragement to support your healing journey. Each chapter provides practical tools and inspiring stories to help you navigate the complexities of your experiences and move toward a life of resilience and empowerment.

Chapter 7: Developing Self-Worth and Identity

Rediscovering and Affirming Self-Worth

Self-worth is the foundation of a healthy and fulfilling life. It is the intrinsic value we assign to ourselves, independent of external achievements, relationships, or validation. For adult children of substance abusers, developing a sense of self-worth can be particularly challenging due to the instability and often negative messages received during their formative years. Rediscovering and affirming self-worth is a crucial step in the journey toward healing and personal growth.

1. Understanding Self-Worth:

SELF-WORTH IS THE BELIEF in one's inherent value and dignity. It is not contingent on external factors such as success, appearance, or approval from others. A strong sense of self-worth provides the foundation for confidence, resilience, and well-being.

2. Recognizing the Impact of Childhood Experiences:

THE EXPERIENCES AND messages received during childhood significantly influence self-worth. In families affected by substance abuse, children often receive inconsistent or negative feedback, leading to feelings of inadequacy, unworthiness, and low self-esteem. Recognizing the impact of these experiences is the first step toward rebuilding self-worth.

3. Challenging Negative Beliefs:

CHALLENGING AND REFRAMING negative beliefs about oneself is essential for affirming self-worth. These beliefs often stem from internalized criticism and negative messages received in childhood. Identifying and challenging these beliefs involves questioning their validity and replacing them with more positive and realistic perspectives.

Steps for Challenging Negative Beliefs:

1. IDENTIFY NEGATIVE beliefs about yourself, such as "I am not good enough" or "I don't deserve love."

2. Examine the evidence for and against these beliefs. Consider whether they are based on facts or assumptions.

3. Replace negative beliefs with positive and supportive statements, such as "I am worthy of love and respect" or "I have valuable strengths and qualities."

4. Repeat positive affirmations regularly to reinforce new, empowering beliefs.

4. Practicing Self-Compassion:

SELF-COMPASSION INVOLVES treating oneself with kindness, understanding, and acceptance. It means recognizing that everyone makes mistakes and experiences difficulties. Practicing self-compassion can reduce self-criticism, enhance self-worth, and promote overall well-being.

Steps for Practicing Self-Compassion:

1. ACKNOWLEDGE YOUR feelings and experiences without judgment.

2. Offer yourself words of comfort and understanding, such as "It's okay to feel this way" or "I am doing my best."

3. Engage in self-care activities that nurture your physical, emotional, and mental well-being.

4. Forgive yourself for past mistakes and recognize that growth is a continuous process.

5. Celebrating Achievements:

CELEBRATING ACHIEVEMENTS, no matter how small, is an important way to affirm self-worth. Recognizing and appreciating your accomplishments reinforces a positive self-image and builds confidence.

Steps for Celebrating Achievements:

1. REFLECT ON YOUR accomplishments, both big and small, and acknowledge the effort and determination involved.

2. Share your achievements with supportive friends or family members who can celebrate with you.

3. Reward yourself with a treat or activity that brings you joy and satisfaction.

4. Keep a journal of your achievements to remind yourself of your progress and growth.

6. Setting and Achieving Personal Goals:

SETTING AND ACHIEVING personal goals can enhance self-worth by providing a sense of purpose and accomplishment. Goals should be realistic, achievable, and aligned with your values and aspirations.

Steps for Setting and Achieving Goals:

1. IDENTIFY SPECIFIC, measurable, achievable, relevant, and time-bound (SMART) goals.

2. Break larger goals into smaller, manageable steps to avoid feeling overwhelmed.

3. Create a plan of action and set deadlines for each step.

4. Track your progress and celebrate milestones along the way.

5. Adjust your goals as needed to stay aligned with your evolving needs and priorities.

7. Engaging in Positive Self-Talk:

POSITIVE SELF-TALK involves replacing negative and self-critical thoughts with encouraging and supportive ones. This practice can help build self-esteem and promote self-worth.

Steps for Engaging in Positive Self-Talk:

1. NOTICE WHEN YOU have negative or self-critical thoughts.

2. Challenge these thoughts by examining the evidence for and against them.

3. Replace negative thoughts with positive and supportive statements, such as "I am capable and strong" or "I deserve happiness and success."

4. Practice positive self-talk regularly to reinforce self-worth and self-confidence.

8. Seeking Support and Validation:

BUILDING SELF-WORTH is often easier with the support and validation of others. Surround yourself with people who appreciate and value you, and seek out relationships that offer encouragement and positive reinforcement.

Steps for Seeking Support and Validation:

1. IDENTIFY INDIVIDUALS who are positive, supportive, and understanding.

2. Communicate openly and honestly with these individuals about your needs and experiences.

3. Engage in activities and spend quality time with supportive friends and family.

4. Join support groups or online communities that focus on self-worth and personal growth.

5. Build a network of supportive relationships that foster mutual respect and understanding.

9. Embracing Authenticity:

EMBRACING AUTHENTICITY involves being true to yourself and aligning your actions with your values and beliefs. Living authentically can enhance self-worth by fostering a sense of integrity and self-respect.

Steps for Embracing Authenticity:

1. REFLECT ON YOUR values, beliefs, and passions to identify what is truly important to you.

2. Make decisions and take actions that align with your authentic self.

3. Communicate honestly and openly with others, expressing your true thoughts and feelings.

4. Surround yourself with people who appreciate and support your authentic self.

5. Embrace your uniqueness and celebrate what makes you special.

Exploring Personal Identity Outside of Family Roles

EXPLORING AND DEFINING your personal identity outside of family roles is essential for developing a strong sense of self and self-worth. This process involves discovering your passions, values, and aspirations independent of familial expectations and dynamics.

1. Understanding the Influence of Family Roles:

FAMILY ROLES OFTEN shape our identity and behavior, especially in families affected by substance abuse. Common roles include the caretaker, the enabler, the scapegoat, the lost child, and the hero. These roles can limit our understanding of ourselves and our potential.

Steps to Understand Family Roles:

1. REFLECT ON THE ROLES you played within your family and how they influenced your behavior and self-perception.

2. Identify the expectations and responsibilities associated with these roles.

3. Consider how these roles may have limited your exploration of other aspects of your identity.

4. Acknowledge the positive and negative impacts of these roles on your development.

2. Identifying Personal Values and Beliefs:

PERSONAL VALUES AND beliefs are the principles and standards that guide our behavior and decision-making. Identifying and aligning with your values is crucial for developing a strong sense of identity.

Steps to Identify Personal Values and Beliefs:

1. REFLECT ON WHAT is most important to you in life, such as integrity, compassion, creativity, or adventure.

2. Consider how your values and beliefs influence your decisions and actions.

3. Write down your core values and beliefs to clarify and affirm them.

4. Align your actions and choices with your identified values and beliefs.

3. Exploring Passions and Interests:

EXPLORING YOUR PASSIONS and interests can help you discover aspects of your identity beyond family roles. Engaging in activities that bring joy and fulfillment can enhance your sense of self and well-being.

Steps to Explore Passions and Interests:

1. REFLECT ON ACTIVITIES and hobbies that you enjoy or have enjoyed in the past.

2. Try new experiences and explore different interests to discover what resonates with you.

3. Engage in activities that bring you joy, satisfaction, and a sense of purpose.

4. Connect with others who share your passions and interests to build supportive relationships.

4. Setting Personal Goals and Aspirations:

SETTING PERSONAL GOALS and aspirations can help you define your identity and create a sense of purpose. These goals should reflect your values, passions, and long-term vision for your life.

Steps to Set Personal Goals and Aspirations:

1. REFLECT ON YOUR long-term vision for your life and what you hope to achieve.

2. Set specific, measurable, achievable, relevant, and time-bound (SMART) goals that align with your vision.

3. Break larger goals into smaller, manageable steps to avoid feeling overwhelmed.

4. Create a plan of action and set deadlines for each step.

5. Track your progress and celebrate milestones along the way.

6. Adjust your goals as needed to stay aligned with your evolving needs and priorities.

5. Embracing Personal Growth and Development:

PERSONAL GROWTH AND development involve continuous learning and self-improvement. Embracing this process can help you discover new aspects of your identity and enhance your self-worth.

Steps to Embrace Personal Growth and Development:

1. IDENTIFY AREAS OF your life where you want to grow and improve.

2. Seek out opportunities for learning and development, such as courses, workshops, or books.

3. Set personal growth goals and create a plan of action to achieve them.

4. Reflect on your progress and celebrate your achievements.

5. Stay open to new experiences and be willing to step outside your comfort zone.

6. Building a Supportive Community:

BUILDING A SUPPORTIVE community of like-minded individuals can provide encouragement and validation as you explore your identity. Surrounding yourself with people who appreciate and support your authentic self can enhance your sense of belonging and self-worth.

Steps to Build a Supportive Community:

1. IDENTIFY INDIVIDUALS who share your values, interests, and passions.

2. Engage in activities and events where you can connect with like-minded people.

3. Foster relationships based on mutual respect, support, and understanding.

4. Communicate openly and honestly with your community about your experiences and aspirations.

5. Seek out mentorship and guidance from individuals who inspire and motivate you.

7. Practicing Self-Reflection:

REGULAR SELF-REFLECTION can help you gain insight into your identity, values, and goals. This practice allows you to evaluate your progress, make adjustments, and stay aligned with your authentic self.

Steps for Practicing Self-Reflection:

1. SET ASIDE REGULAR time for self-reflection, such as daily journaling or weekly meditation.

2. Reflect on your experiences, decisions, and actions, considering how they align with your values and goals.

3. Identify areas of growth and improvement, and set intentions for positive change.

4. Celebrate your achievements and progress, acknowledging your efforts and determination.

5. Stay open to new insights and perspectives that can enhance your understanding of yourself.

Building a Positive Self-Image

BUILDING A POSITIVE self-image involves cultivating a healthy and empowering view of oneself. It requires challenging negative self-perceptions, embracing your strengths and uniqueness, and fostering self-love and acceptance.

1. Challenging Negative Self-Perceptions:

NEGATIVE SELF-PERCEPTIONS often stem from internalized criticism and negative messages received in childhood. Challenging and reframing these perceptions is essential for building a positive self-image.

Steps to Challenge Negative Self-Perceptions:

1. IDENTIFY NEGATIVE self-perceptions, such as "I am not good enough" or "I am unlovable."

2. Examine the evidence for and against these perceptions, considering whether they are based on facts or assumptions.

3. Replace negative self-perceptions with positive and supportive statements, such as "I am capable and worthy" or "I deserve love and respect."

4. Repeat positive affirmations regularly to reinforce new, empowering self-perceptions.

2. Embracing Strengths and Uniqueness:

EMBRACING YOUR STRENGTHS and uniqueness involves recognizing and celebrating the qualities that make you special. This practice can enhance your self-esteem and promote a positive self-image.

Steps to Embrace Strengths and Uniqueness:

1. REFLECT ON YOUR strengths, talents, and positive qualities.

2. Write down a list of your strengths and qualities to affirm and celebrate them.

3. Seek out opportunities to use and develop your strengths and talents.

4. Embrace your uniqueness and celebrate what makes you different from others.

5. Surround yourself with people who appreciate and support your strengths and uniqueness.

3. Practicing Self-Love and Acceptance:

SELF-LOVE AND ACCEPTANCE involve treating yourself with kindness, understanding, and compassion. It means embracing all aspects of yourself, including your imperfections and flaws.

Steps to Practice Self-Love and Acceptance:

1. ACKNOWLEDGE YOUR feelings and experiences without judgment.

2. Offer yourself words of comfort and understanding, such as "I am worthy of love and acceptance" or "I am enough just as I am."

3. Engage in self-care activities that nurture your physical, emotional, and mental well-being.

4. Forgive yourself for past mistakes and recognize that growth is a continuous process.

5. Celebrate your achievements and progress, acknowledging your efforts and determination.

4. Engaging in Positive Self-Talk:

POSITIVE SELF-TALK involves replacing negative and self-critical thoughts with encouraging and supportive ones. This practice can help build self-esteem and promote a positive self-image.

Steps for Engaging in Positive Self-Talk:

1. NOTICE WHEN YOU have negative or self-critical thoughts.

2. Challenge these thoughts by examining the evidence for and against them.

3. Replace negative thoughts with positive and supportive statements, such as "I am capable and strong" or "I deserve happiness and success."

4. Practice positive self-talk regularly to reinforce self-worth and self-confidence.

5. Cultivating Gratitude:

PRACTICING GRATITUDE involves regularly reflecting on and appreciating the positive aspects of your life. This practice can help shift focus from negative to positive and foster a sense of self-love and contentment.

Steps for Cultivating Gratitude:

1. SET ASIDE TIME EACH day to reflect on things you are grateful for.

2. Write down three to five things you appreciate about yourself and your life.

3. Reflect on these aspects and allow yourself to feel the gratitude and appreciation.

4. Consider expressing gratitude to others, whether through a note, a conversation, or an act of kindness.

5. Practice gratitude regularly to cultivate a positive mindset and self-love.

6. Seeking Feedback and Validation:

SEEKING FEEDBACK AND validation from others can provide valuable insights and reinforce a positive self-image. Surround yourself with people who offer constructive feedback and encouragement.

Steps for Seeking Feedback and Validation:

1. IDENTIFY INDIVIDUALS who are positive, supportive, and understanding.

2. Communicate openly and honestly with these individuals about your needs and experiences.

3. Seek out feedback on your strengths, talents, and areas of growth.

4. Use the feedback to reinforce your positive self-image and make improvements as needed.

5. Express gratitude for the feedback and validation received.

7. Embracing Personal Growth and Development:

PERSONAL GROWTH AND development involve continuous learning and self-improvement. Embracing this process can help you discover new aspects of your identity and enhance your self-worth.

Steps to Embrace Personal Growth and Development:

1. IDENTIFY AREAS OF your life where you want to grow and improve.

2. Seek out opportunities for learning and development, such as courses, workshops, or books.

3. Set personal growth goals and create a plan of action to achieve them.

4. Reflect on your progress and celebrate your achievements.

5. Stay open to new experiences and be willing to step outside your comfort zone.

8. Building a Supportive Community:

BUILDING A SUPPORTIVE community of like-minded individuals can provide encouragement and validation as you explore your identity. Surrounding yourself with people who appreciate and support your authentic self can enhance your sense of belonging and self-worth.

Steps to Build a Supportive Community:

1. IDENTIFY INDIVIDUALS who share your values, interests, and passions.

2. Engage in activities and events where you can connect with like-minded people.

3. Foster relationships based on mutual respect, support, and understanding.

4. Communicate openly and honestly with your community about your experiences and aspirations.

5. Seek out mentorship and guidance from individuals who inspire and motivate you.

9. Practicing Self-Reflection:

REGULAR SELF-REFLECTION can help you gain insight into your identity, values, and goals. This practice allows you to evaluate your progress, make adjustments, and stay aligned with your authentic self.

Steps for Practicing Self-Reflection:

1. SET ASIDE REGULAR time for self-reflection, such as daily journaling or weekly meditation.

2. Reflect on your experiences, decisions, and actions, considering how they align with your values and goals.

3. Identify areas of growth and improvement, and set intentions for positive change.

4. Celebrate your achievements and progress, acknowledging your efforts and determination.

5. Stay open to new insights and perspectives that can enhance your understanding of yourself.

Conclusion

Developing self-worth and identity is a journey of self-discovery, compassion, and growth. Rediscovering and affirming self-worth, exploring personal identity outside of family roles, and building a positive self-image are essential steps in this process. By implementing the techniques and exercises outlined in this chapter, you can reconnect with your true self, heal past wounds, and create a fulfilling and joyful life.

Remember that healing and growth take time and effort. Be patient and compassionate with yourself as you navigate this journey. Seek support when needed, prioritize your well-being, and celebrate your progress and growth. By taking these steps, you can embrace your authentic self and move toward a life of resilience, empowerment, and self-love.

As you continue reading this book, you will find additional insights, strategies, and encouragement to support your healing journey. Each chapter provides practical tools and inspiring stories to help you navigate the complexities of your experiences and move toward a life of resilience and empowerment.

Chapter 8: Communication Skills for Conflict Resolution

Effective Communication Techniques

Effective communication is the cornerstone of resolving conflicts, particularly within families. Misunderstandings, assumptions, and emotional triggers often exacerbate conflicts, making effective communication essential for clarity, empathy, and resolution.

1. Active Listening:

ACTIVE LISTENING INVOLVES fully concentrating on what the other person is saying without interrupting or planning your response while they are speaking. It requires attention, patience, and empathy.

Steps for Active Listening:

1. FOCUS: GIVE THE speaker your full attention, maintaining eye contact and showing interest through nods or verbal affirmations like "I see" or "I understand."

2. Reflect: Paraphrase or summarize what the speaker has said to confirm your understanding. For example, "So what I hear you saying is..."

3. Clarify: Ask open-ended questions to gain more information and understanding. For instance, "Can you explain more about how that made you feel?"

4. Validate: Acknowledge the speaker's feelings and perspective without judgment. Statements like "That sounds really challenging" or "I can see why you feel that way" can help.

2. Nonverbal Communication:

NONVERBAL COMMUNICATION includes body language, facial expressions, gestures, posture, and tone of voice. It can significantly impact how messages are received and interpreted.

Tips for Effective Nonverbal Communication:

1. MAINTAIN EYE CONTACT: This shows that you are engaged and paying attention.

2. Open Body Language: Avoid crossing your arms or legs, which can appear defensive. Instead, keep an open posture.

3. Facial Expressions: Ensure your facial expressions match your words to avoid mixed messages.

4. Tone of Voice: Use a calm, respectful tone, even when discussing difficult topics.

3. "I" Statements:

Using "I" statements instead of "You" statements helps express your feelings without blaming or accusing the other person, which can reduce defensiveness.

Examples of "I" Statements:

- INSTEAD OF SAYING, "You never listen to me," try, "I feel unheard when I don't get a chance to share my thoughts."

- Instead of saying, "You always make decisions without me," try, "I feel excluded when decisions are made without my input."

4. Empathy and Compassion:

EMPATHY INVOLVES UNDERSTANDING and sharing the feelings of another person. Compassion takes empathy a step further by also wanting to help alleviate their suffering.

Practicing Empathy and Compassion:

1. PUT YOURSELF IN Their Shoes: Try to see the situation from the other person's perspective.

2. Express Understanding: Verbalize your understanding of their feelings. "I can see why you would feel upset about that."

3. Show Support: Offer support or assistance if appropriate. "How can I help you through this?"

5. Clear and Concise Messaging:

BEING CLEAR AND CONCISE helps avoid misunderstandings and ensures that your message is received as intended.

Tips for Clear and Concise Communication:

1. BE DIRECT: STATE your main point early in the conversation.

2. Use Simple Language: Avoid jargon or overly complex language.

3. Stay on Topic: Focus on the issue at hand without bringing up unrelated topics or past conflicts.

6. Timing and Setting:

CHOOSING THE RIGHT time and place for a conversation can greatly influence its outcome. Avoid discussing sensitive topics when either party is tired, stressed, or distracted.

Tips for Choosing Timing and Setting:

1. SELECT A CALM ENVIRONMENT: Choose a quiet, private place free from interruptions.

2. Consider Timing: Ensure both parties are in a calm and receptive state of mind.

3. Set the Tone: Begin with a positive or neutral statement to set a constructive tone for the conversation.

Dealing with Difficult Conversations

DIFFICULT CONVERSATIONS are inevitable in any relationship, especially within families. Handling these conversations effectively requires preparation, emotional regulation, and a focus on mutual respect and understanding.

1. Preparing for the Conversation:

PREPARATION CAN HELP you approach difficult conversations with confidence and clarity.

Steps for Preparing:

1. IDENTIFY THE ISSUE: Clearly define the issue you want to discuss.

2. Know Your Goal: Understand what you hope to achieve from the conversation.

3. Consider the Other Person's Perspective: Think about how the other person might feel and what their concerns might be.

4. Plan Your Approach: Decide how you will introduce the topic and what points you want to cover.

2. Emotional Regulation:

MANAGING YOUR EMOTIONS is crucial during difficult conversations to maintain calm and composure.

Techniques for Emotional Regulation:

1. DEEP BREATHING: Practice deep breathing exercises to stay calm.

2. Mindfulness: Focus on the present moment and your physical sensations to stay grounded.

3. Pause: If you feel overwhelmed, take a moment to pause and collect your thoughts before responding.

3. Starting the Conversation:

HOW YOU BEGIN THE CONVERSATION can set the tone for the entire discussion.

Tips for Starting the Conversation:

1. USE A GENTLE START-Up: Begin with a neutral or positive statement. "I appreciate you taking the time to talk with me."

2. State Your Intention: Clearly state why you want to have the conversation. "I want to discuss something that's been bothering me so we can find a solution together."

3. Express Empathy: Acknowledge the other person's feelings. "I know this might be a difficult topic to discuss, but I value our relationship."

4. Navigating the Conversation:

DURING THE CONVERSATION, aim to maintain a collaborative and respectful approach.

Strategies for Navigating the Conversation:

1. STAY FOCUSED: KEEP the conversation on the current issue without bringing up past conflicts.

2. Avoid Blame: Use "I" statements and focus on your feelings and needs rather than blaming the other person.

3. Listen Actively: Show that you are listening and understanding the other person's perspective.

4. Seek Common Ground: Look for areas of agreement and shared goals.

5. Managing Disagreements:

DISAGREEMENTS ARE NATURAL, but how you handle them can make a difference in the outcome of the conversation.

Tips for Managing Disagreements:

1. STAY CALM: KEEP your emotions in check and avoid raising your voice.

2. Acknowledge Differences: Respectfully acknowledge that you may have different perspectives. "I see that we have different views on this."

3. Focus on Solutions: Shift the focus from the disagreement to finding a solution. "How can we work together to resolve this?"

6. Ending the Conversation:

ENDING THE CONVERSATION on a positive note can help maintain goodwill and pave the way for future discussions.

Steps for Ending the Conversation:

1. SUMMARIZE: RECAP the main points and any agreements made. "So, we agreed to..."

2. Express Gratitude: Thank the other person for their time and willingness to discuss the issue. "Thank you for talking with me about this."

3. Plan Next Steps: If needed, plan a follow-up conversation or outline next steps. "Let's check in again next week to see how things are going."

Strategies for Conflict Resolution Within the Family

CONFLICT WITHIN FAMILIES is inevitable, but it doesn't have to be destructive. Effective conflict resolution involves addressing issues constructively, fostering understanding, and finding mutually acceptable solutions.

1. Understanding Conflict Dynamics:

UNDERSTANDING THE DYNAMICS of conflict can help you approach resolution more effectively.

Key Elements of Conflict Dynamics:

1. UNDERLYING ISSUES: Identify the root causes of the conflict, such as unmet needs, miscommunication, or differing values.

2. Emotional Triggers: Recognize the emotions involved and how they influence behavior and responses.

3. Power Dynamics: Be aware of any power imbalances and how they impact the conflict.

2. Creating a Safe Environment:

CREATING A SAFE AND respectful environment is essential for productive conflict resolution.

Steps for Creating a Safe Environment:

1. ESTABLISH GROUND Rules: Set rules for respectful communication, such as no interrupting, no name-calling, and allowing each person to speak.

2. Ensure Privacy: Choose a private setting where everyone feels comfortable to speak openly.

3. Encourage Participation: Encourage all parties involved to share their perspectives and contribute to the discussion.

3. Identifying and Addressing Underlying Issues:

ADDRESSING THE UNDERLYING issues is crucial for resolving conflicts effectively.

Steps for Identifying and Addressing Underlying Issues:

1. LISTEN ACTIVELY: Listen to understand the other person's perspective and identify their underlying concerns.

2. Ask Open-Ended Questions: Ask questions that encourage the other person to elaborate on their feelings and needs. "Can you tell me more about why this is important to you?"

3. Validate Feelings: Acknowledge and validate the other person's emotions and concerns. "I understand that you feel upset about this."

4. Explore Solutions Together: Collaborate to find solutions that address the underlying issues. "What can we do to resolve this issue?"

4. Using Mediation and Facilitation:

MEDIATION AND FACILITATION can be effective tools for resolving family conflicts, especially when emotions run high or communication breaks down.

Steps for Mediation and Facilitation:

1. INVOLVE A NEUTRAL Third Party: A mediator or facilitator can help guide the discussion and ensure all voices are heard.

2. Set Clear Objectives: Define the goals of the mediation, such as finding a mutually acceptable solution or improving communication.

3. Follow a Structured Process: Use a structured process to address the conflict, such as opening statements, issue exploration, and solution brainstorming.

4. Focus on Collaboration: Encourage collaboration and compromise to reach a resolution that satisfies all parties.

5. Practicing Forgiveness and Letting Go:

FORGIVENESS AND LETTING go of past grievances are essential for moving forward and maintaining healthy family relationships.

Steps for Practicing Forgiveness and Letting Go:

1. ACKNOWLEDGE THE Hurt: Recognize and acknowledge the hurt and impact of the conflict.

2. Express Your Feelings: Share your feelings and experiences with the other person, if appropriate.

3. Choose to Forgive: Make a conscious decision to forgive the other person, even if you do not condone their behavior.

4. Let Go of Resentment: Release any lingering resentment or desire for revenge.

5. Focus on the Future: Shift your focus from past grievances to building a positive and healthy relationship moving forward.

6. Maintaining Healthy Communication:

MAINTAINING HEALTHY communication is crucial for preventing conflicts and fostering positive family relationships.

Tips for Maintaining Healthy Communication:

1. REGULAR CHECK-INS: Schedule regular check-ins to discuss any issues or concerns before they escalate into conflicts.

2. Practice Active Listening: Continuously practice active listening to understand and validate each other's perspectives.

3. Use "I" Statements: Continue to use "I" statements to express your feelings and needs without blaming or accusing.

4. Respect Boundaries: Respect each other's boundaries and personal space to maintain a sense of safety and respect.

5. Seek Professional Help: If conflicts persist or become overwhelming, seek the help of a family therapist or counselor.

Conclusion

Developing effective communication skills is essential for resolving conflicts within the family. By practicing active listening, using "I" statements, and maintaining a respectful and empathetic approach, you can navigate difficult conversations and find mutually acceptable solutions. Understanding conflict dynamics, creating a safe environment, and addressing underlying issues are crucial for resolving conflicts constructively.

Remember that conflict resolution is an ongoing process that requires patience, effort, and a commitment to healthy communication. Be patient and compassionate with yourself and others as you navigate this journey. Seek support when needed, prioritize your well-being, and celebrate your progress and growth. By taking these steps, you can foster positive family relationships and create a more harmonious and resilient family dynamic.

As you continue reading this book, you will find additional insights, strategies, and encouragement to support your healing journey. Each chapter provides practical tools and inspiring stories to help you navigate the complexities of your experiences and move toward a life of resilience and empowerment.

Chapter 9: The Role of Therapy and Support Groups

Benefits of Professional Help

Professional help, including therapy and support groups, plays a crucial role in the healing process for adult children of substance abusers. Engaging with professional support provides a structured environment to explore and address the deep-seated issues stemming from growing up in a household affected by addiction.

1. Safe and Nonjudgmental Space:

THERAPISTS PROVIDE a safe and nonjudgmental space where individuals can openly discuss their experiences, feelings, and thoughts without fear of criticism or reprisal. This environment fosters trust and allows for honest self-exploration.

2. Professional Expertise:

THERAPISTS ARE TRAINED professionals with expertise in mental health and emotional well-being. They possess the skills and knowledge to identify and address various psychological issues, such as trauma, anxiety, depression, and low self-esteem. Their guidance can help individuals develop healthy coping mechanisms and emotional regulation strategies.

3. Tailored Treatment Plans:

PROFESSIONAL THERAPISTS develop tailored treatment plans based on individual needs and circumstances. These personalized plans ensure that therapy addresses specific issues and goals, making the process more effective and efficient.

4. Emotional Support and Validation:

THERAPISTS OFFER EMOTIONAL support and validation, helping individuals feel understood and accepted. This validation is particularly important for those who have experienced neglect, abuse, or invalidation during their upbringing.

5. Healing from Trauma:

MANY ADULT CHILDREN of substance abusers carry unresolved trauma from their childhood. Therapists can employ various therapeutic techniques, such as cognitive-behavioral therapy (CBT), eye movement desensitization and reprocessing (EMDR), and trauma-focused therapy, to help individuals process and heal from their traumatic experiences.

6. Improved Self-Awareness:

THERAPY ENCOURAGES self-reflection and introspection, leading to greater self-awareness. Understanding the root causes of emotional and behavioral patterns empowers individuals to make positive changes in their lives.

7. Development of Healthy Relationships:

THERAPISTS CAN HELP individuals improve their interpersonal skills and build healthy relationships. By exploring attachment styles and communication patterns, therapy can enhance relationship dynamics and foster more meaningful connections.

8. Coping Skills and Strategies:

THERAPY EQUIPS INDIVIDUALS with practical coping skills and strategies to manage stress, anxiety, and other emotional challenges. These tools are essential for navigating everyday life and maintaining mental well-being.

9. Prevention of Intergenerational Trauma:

ENGAGING IN THERAPY can help break the cycle of intergenerational trauma. By addressing and healing from their own experiences, individuals can create healthier environments for their children and future generations.

10. Enhanced Quality of Life:

OVERALL, THERAPY CAN significantly enhance an individual's quality of life. It promotes emotional healing, personal growth, and resilience, enabling individuals to lead more fulfilling and empowered lives.

Finding the Right Therapist or Support Group

FINDING THE RIGHT THERAPIST or support group is a crucial step in the healing journey. It involves identifying professionals and groups that align with individual needs, preferences, and goals.

1. Identifying Needs and Goals:

BEFORE SEEKING A THERAPIST or support group, it is essential to identify your specific needs and goals. Consider the following questions:

- What issues or challenges do I want to address in therapy?

- What type of therapeutic approach am I comfortable with?

- Do I prefer individual therapy, group therapy, or a combination of both?

- What are my goals for therapy or support group participation?

2. Researching Therapists:

RESEARCHING POTENTIAL therapists involves gathering information about their qualifications, experience, and therapeutic approaches.

Steps for Researching Therapists:

1. CREDENTIALS AND Licenses: Ensure the therapist is licensed and has the necessary credentials to practice. Look for certifications in relevant areas, such as trauma therapy or addiction counseling.

2. Experience: Consider the therapist's experience working with individuals who have similar backgrounds or issues. A therapist with experience in dealing with adult children of substance abusers can offer valuable insights and tailored support.

3. Therapeutic Approaches: Different therapists use various therapeutic approaches, such as CBT, EMDR, psychodynamic therapy, and humanistic therapy. Research these approaches to determine which aligns with your preferences and needs.

4. Reviews and Recommendations: Read reviews and seek recommendations from trusted sources, such as friends, family, or healthcare providers. Personal experiences can provide valuable insights into the therapist's effectiveness and approach.

5. Initial Consultation: Many therapists offer initial consultations to discuss your needs and goals. Use this opportunity to ask questions, assess compatibility, and determine if you feel comfortable with the therapist.

3. Exploring Support Groups:

SUPPORT GROUPS OFFER a sense of community and shared experience, providing valuable emotional support and practical advice.

Types of Support Groups:

1. 12-STEP PROGRAMS: Programs such as Al-Anon and Adult Children of Alcoholics (ACA) follow a structured, 12-step approach to recovery and support. These groups provide a framework for addressing the impact of a parent's addiction and fostering personal growth.

2. Therapist-Led Groups: These groups are facilitated by a licensed therapist and offer a combination of support and therapeutic intervention. They often focus on specific issues, such as trauma, anxiety, or relationship dynamics.

3. Peer Support Groups: Peer-led groups consist of individuals with similar experiences who come together to share stories, provide support, and offer practical advice. These groups foster a sense of camaraderie and mutual understanding.

Steps for Finding the Right Support Group:

1. IDENTIFY YOUR NEEDS: Determine what you hope to gain from a support group, such as emotional support, practical advice, or a sense of community.

2. Research Options: Look for support groups in your area or online. Consider factors such as the group's focus, format (in-person or virtual), and meeting frequency.

3. Attend a Meeting: Attend a few meetings to assess the group's dynamics, structure, and whether it meets your needs. Pay attention to how comfortable you feel and whether the group provides the support you are seeking.

4. Evaluate Compatibility: Consider whether the group's approach and atmosphere align with your preferences and goals. Trust your instincts and choose a group where you feel supported and understood.

4. Financial Considerations:

FINANCIAL CONSIDERATIONS are an important aspect of finding the right therapist or support group. Therapy and support group fees can vary widely.

Options for Affordable Therapy:

1. INSURANCE COVERAGE: Check if your health insurance plan covers therapy sessions. Many plans include mental health benefits that can reduce out-of-pocket costs.

2. Sliding Scale Fees: Some therapists offer sliding scale fees based on income. Inquire about this option during the initial consultation.

3. Community Clinics: Community mental health clinics often provide low-cost or free therapy services. Research local clinics to find affordable options.

4. Online Therapy: Online therapy platforms can offer more affordable rates compared to in-person therapy. These platforms connect you with licensed therapists for virtual sessions.

5. Support Groups: Many support groups, especially peer-led and 12-step programs, are free or request a small donation.

5. Building a Support Network:

BUILDING A SUPPORT network involves combining therapy and support groups with other sources of support, such as friends, family, and online communities.

Steps for Building a Support Network:

1. ENGAGE WITH MULTIPLE Sources: Utilize a combination of therapy, support groups, and personal relationships to create a comprehensive support network.

2. Communicate Openly: Share your experiences and needs with trusted individuals in your network. Open communication fosters understanding and support.

3. Participate Actively: Engage actively in therapy and support groups to maximize the benefits. Consistent participation enhances the support you receive.

4. Seek Ongoing Support: Recognize that support needs may evolve over time. Continuously seek out and engage with resources that align with your changing needs.

Personal Stories of Recovery and Growth

PERSONAL STORIES OF recovery and growth provide inspiration, hope, and practical insights for others on their healing journey. These stories highlight the transformative power of therapy and support groups and demonstrate the resilience and strength of individuals who have navigated the challenges of growing up with a substance-abusing parent.

Story 1: Emma's Journey to Self-Discovery

EMMA GREW UP IN A HOUSEHOLD marked by her father's alcoholism. As the eldest of three siblings, she often found herself in the caretaker role, managing household responsibilities and trying to shield her younger siblings from their father's erratic behavior. Emma's childhood was characterized by constant anxiety and a pervasive sense of inadequacy.

Seeking Help:

IN HER LATE TWENTIES, Emma recognized that her childhood experiences were affecting her adult life. She struggled with low self-esteem, difficulty trusting others, and a deep-seated fear of abandonment. Encouraged by a close friend, Emma decided to seek therapy.

Therapeutic Journey:

EMMA'S THERAPIST SPECIALIZED in trauma and family dynamics. Through their sessions, Emma began to unpack the impact of her father's alcoholism on her self-worth and relationships. They used a combination of CBT and EMDR to address her traumatic memories and develop healthier coping mechanisms.

Support Group Involvement:

IN ADDITION TO THERAPY, Emma joined a local Al-Anon group. The sense of community and shared experiences provided Emma with invaluable support and validation. Hearing others' stories helped her feel less isolated and more understood.

Transformation and Growth:

OVER TIME, EMMA EXPERIENCED significant personal growth. She learned to set healthy boundaries, build trust in her relationships, and develop a strong sense of self-worth. Emma's journey was not without challenges, but her commitment to therapy and support groups empowered her to overcome them. Today, Emma works as a social worker, helping others navigate similar challenges and find their path to healing.

Story 2: James' Path to Emotional Resilience

JAMES GREW UP WITH a mother who struggled with prescription drug addiction. As a child, he often felt neglected and invisible, his emotional needs overshadowed by his mother's addiction. James coped by withdrawing emotionally and avoiding close relationships.

Seeking Help:

IN HIS THIRTIES, JAMES realized that his emotional detachment was affecting his marriage and his ability to connect with his children. At his wife's urging, James sought therapy to address his unresolved childhood issues.

Therapeutic Journey:

JAMES FOUND A THERAPIST who specialized in attachment theory and trauma. Through therapy, James explored his childhood experiences and their impact on his adult behavior. His therapist used psychodynamic therapy to help James understand and process his emotions.

Support Group Involvement:

JAMES ALSO JOINED AN ACA group, where he connected with others who had similar experiences. The group provided a safe space for James to share his story and receive support. The shared understanding and empathy helped James feel less alone in his struggles.

Transformation and Growth:

WITH TIME AND DEDICATION, James began to open up emotionally and build stronger connections with his family. He learned to express his feelings, set boundaries, and develop healthier relationship patterns. James's journey taught him the importance of emotional resilience and the power of community support. Today, he volunteers as a facilitator for his ACA group, helping others find their voice and path to healing.

Story 3: Lily's Road to Self-Acceptance

LILY'S CHILDHOOD WAS marked by her mother's addiction to alcohol and her father's enabling behavior. Lily often felt responsible for her mother's well-being and struggled with feelings of guilt and shame. She developed perfectionistic tendencies, believing that if she were "perfect," she could somehow fix her family's problems.

Seeking Help:

IN HER LATE TWENTIES, Lily's perfectionism and anxiety became overwhelming. She realized that her coping mechanisms were no longer sustainable and decided to seek therapy.

Therapeutic Journey:

LILY'S THERAPIST USED a combination of humanistic therapy and mindfulness-based techniques. Together, they worked on addressing Lily's perfectionism, guilt, and self-criticism. The therapist helped Lily practice self-compassion and develop a more balanced view of herself.

Support Group Involvement:

Lily also joined a therapist-led support group for adult children of alcoholics. The group provided a supportive environment where Lily could share her experiences and learn from others. The therapist-led format offered both peer support and professional guidance.

Transformation and Growth:

THROUGH THERAPY AND the support group, Lily gradually let go of her need for perfection and embraced her authentic self. She learned to set boundaries, prioritize self-care, and practice self-acceptance. Lily's journey was transformative, allowing her to build a life rooted in self-love and authenticity. Today, Lily is a successful artist, using her creative talents to express her journey and inspire others.

Story 4: David's Quest for Inner Peace

DAVID GREW UP IN A volatile environment, with a father who was addicted to drugs and a mother who struggled with depression. The instability and chaos of his childhood left David with deep-seated anger and a tendency to lash out when feeling threatened or vulnerable.

Seeking Help:

IN HIS EARLY FORTIES, David's anger issues began to affect his career and personal relationships. Realizing the need for change, he decided to seek therapy to address his unresolved anger and trauma.

Therapeutic Journey:

DAVID'S THERAPIST SPECIALIZED in anger management and trauma therapy. Through their sessions, David explored the root causes of his anger and developed healthier ways to express and manage his emotions. They used techniques such as mindfulness, deep breathing, and CBT to help David regulate his anger.

Support Group Involvement:

DAVID ALSO JOINED A support group for men dealing with anger issues. The group provided a safe space for David to share his experiences and learn from others. The camaraderie and mutual support helped David feel less isolated in his struggles.

Transformation and Growth:

WITH THE SUPPORT OF therapy and the group, David experienced significant growth. He learned to recognize his anger triggers, communicate more effectively, and practice self-compassion. David's journey taught him the importance of inner peace and emotional regulation. Today, he works as a motivational speaker, sharing his story and helping others find their path to healing.

Conclusion

Therapy and support groups play a pivotal role in the recovery and growth of adult children of substance abusers. The benefits of professional help, including emotional support, tailored treatment plans, and the development of healthy coping mechanisms, are invaluable. Finding the right therapist or support group involves identifying individual needs, researching options, and building a comprehensive support network.

Personal stories of recovery and growth highlight the transformative power of therapy and support groups. These stories demonstrate the resilience and strength of individuals who have navigated the challenges of growing up with a substance-abusing parent and found their path to healing and empowerment.

As you continue reading this book, you will find additional insights, strategies, and encouragement to support your healing journey. Each chapter provides practical tools and inspiring stories to help you navigate the complexities of your experiences and move toward a life of resilience and empowerment. Remember, healing is a journey, and seeking support is a courageous and vital step toward a healthier, more fulfilling life.

Chapter 10: Overcoming Codependency

Understanding Codependency and Its Signs

Codependency is a complex behavioral condition often rooted in relationships where one person enables another's addiction, poor mental health, immaturity, irresponsibility, or underachievement. It is characterized by excessive emotional or psychological reliance on a partner, typically one who requires support due to an illness or addiction. To effectively overcome codependency, it's essential to first understand its nature, signs, and underlying causes.

1. Definition of Codependency:

CODEPENDENCY INVOLVES a dysfunctional relationship pattern where one person is excessively reliant on another for their emotional needs, often to the detriment of their own well-being. This reliance typically involves enabling behaviors that perpetuate the partner's unhealthy behaviors or dependencies.

2. Origin and Development:

CODEPENDENCY OFTEN develops in dysfunctional families where members fail to meet each other's emotional needs. It is particularly common in families affected by addiction, mental illness, or chronic stress. Children in such environments may learn to prioritize others' needs over their own, internalizing the belief that their worth is tied to their ability to care for or control others.

3. Key Characteristics of Codependency:

- LOW SELF-ESTEEM: CODEPENDENT individuals often have a poor self-image and derive their self-worth from the approval and validation of others.

- People-Pleasing: They have a strong desire to please others and fear rejection or abandonment, leading to difficulty saying no or setting boundaries.

- Caretaking: Codependents frequently take on the role of caregiver, feeling responsible for others' problems and emotions.

- Control Issues: They may attempt to control others' behavior to feel secure, often through manipulation or passive-aggressive tactics.

- Denial: Codependents often deny their own needs and feelings, focusing instead on those of others.

- Dependency: They rely heavily on others for their sense of identity and purpose, struggling with feelings of emptiness when alone.

- Fear of Abandonment: There is a pervasive fear of being alone or abandoned, leading to clingy or overly accommodating behavior.

- Difficulty with Intimacy: Codependents may struggle with true intimacy, as their relationships are often based on neediness and control rather than mutual respect and equality.

4. Signs of Codependency:

RECOGNIZING THE SIGNS of codependency is the first step towards overcoming it. Common signs include:

- Excessive Worrying: Constantly worrying about others and feeling responsible for their well-being.

- Neglecting Self: Ignoring or sacrificing one's own needs, desires, and well-being to care for others.

- Resentment: Feeling unappreciated or resentful when others do not reciprocate care or attention.

- Obsessive Thinking: Being preoccupied with thoughts about another person and their problems.

- Difficulty Saying No: Struggling to set boundaries and say no, even when it's detrimental to oneself.

- Feeling Trapped: Feeling stuck in unhealthy relationships but fearing change or being alone.

- Mood Swings: Experiencing emotional highs and lows based on others' behaviors and reactions.

Breaking Free from Codependent Behaviors

BREAKING FREE FROM codependent behaviors involves recognizing and addressing the underlying patterns and beliefs that perpetuate them. This process requires self-awareness, self-compassion, and a commitment to personal growth and healing.

1. Acknowledging Codependency:

THE FIRST STEP IN OVERCOMING codependency is acknowledging its presence in your life. This involves honest self-reflection and acceptance of the ways in which codependent behaviors have affected your relationships and well-being.

Steps for Acknowledging Codependency:

1. SELF-REFLECTION: Reflect on your relationship patterns and behaviors. Consider how often you prioritize others' needs over your own and the impact this has on your well-being.

2. Identify Patterns: Look for recurring patterns in your relationships, such as people-pleasing, caretaking, and difficulty setting boundaries.

3. Accept Responsibility: Accept responsibility for your role in these patterns without blaming yourself. Recognize that these behaviors developed as coping mechanisms in response to past experiences.

2. Understanding Underlying Causes:

UNDERSTANDING THE UNDERLYING causes of codependency can provide valuable insights and facilitate healing.

Exploring Underlying Causes:

1. FAMILY DYNAMICS: Examine your family dynamics and upbringing. Consider how your parents or caregivers modeled relationships and how their behaviors influenced your own.

2. Trauma and Abuse: Reflect on any traumatic or abusive experiences that may have contributed to your codependent behaviors. Trauma can significantly impact one's ability to form healthy relationships.

3. Attachment Styles: Consider your attachment style and how it affects your relationships. Insecure attachment styles, such as anxious or avoidant attachment, often contribute to codependent behaviors.

3. Developing Self-Awareness:

INCREASING SELF-AWARENESS is crucial for recognizing and changing codependent behaviors.

Techniques for Developing Self-Awareness:

1. MINDFULNESS: PRACTICE mindfulness to become more aware of your thoughts, feelings, and behaviors in the present moment. Mindfulness can help you recognize when you are engaging in codependent behaviors.

2. Journaling: Keep a journal to explore your thoughts, feelings, and relationship patterns. Writing can provide clarity and insight into your behaviors and motivations.

3. Therapy: Seek therapy to explore the underlying causes of your codependency and develop greater self-awareness. A therapist can provide valuable guidance and support.

4. Setting Boundaries:

SETTING AND MAINTAINING healthy boundaries is essential for breaking free from codependency.

Steps for Setting Boundaries:

1. IDENTIFY NEEDS: Reflect on your needs and limits in relationships. Consider what makes you feel safe, respected, and valued.

2. Communicate Clearly: Communicate your boundaries clearly and assertively. Use "I" statements to express your needs and limits.

3. Enforce Boundaries: Consistently enforce your boundaries and follow through with consequences if they are violated. Consistency reinforces the importance of your boundaries.

4. Respect Others' Boundaries: Respect and honor the boundaries of others. Recognize that boundaries are mutual and essential for healthy relationships.

5. Building Self-Esteem:

BUILDING SELF-ESTEEM involves developing a positive self-image and recognizing your intrinsic worth.

Steps for Building Self-Esteem:

1. SELF-COMPASSION: Practice self-compassion by treating yourself with kindness, understanding, and acceptance. Recognize that you are worthy of love and respect.

2. Affirmations: Use positive affirmations to challenge negative self-beliefs and reinforce your self-worth. Repeat affirmations such as "I am worthy of love and respect" or "I deserve to take care of myself."

3. Celebrate Achievements: Acknowledge and celebrate your achievements and successes, no matter how small. Recognize the effort and determination involved.

4. Self-Care: Engage in self-care activities that nurture your physical, emotional, and mental well-being. Prioritize your needs and well-being.

6. Developing Independence:

DEVELOPING INDEPENDENCE involves cultivating a sense of self-sufficiency and autonomy.

Steps for Developing Independence:

1. PURSUE INTERESTS: Engage in activities and hobbies that bring you joy and fulfillment. Explore new interests and passions that are independent of your relationships.

2. Set Goals: Set personal goals and work towards achieving them. Focus on your aspirations and what you want to accomplish in your life.

3. Build Skills: Develop skills that enhance your independence and self-sufficiency. This could include financial management, career development, or self-care practices.

4. Spend Time Alone: Spend time alone to reflect, recharge, and connect with yourself. Embrace solitude as an opportunity for self-discovery and growth.

7. Seeking Support:

SEEKING SUPPORT FROM others is crucial for breaking free from codependency. Surround yourself with individuals who understand and support your journey.

Sources of Support:

1. THERAPISTS AND COUNSELORS: Seek therapy to explore and address codependent behaviors. A therapist can provide guidance, support, and tools for personal growth.

2. Support Groups: Join support groups for codependency, such as Codependents Anonymous (CoDA), to connect with others who share similar experiences. Support groups provide a sense of community and mutual understanding.

3. Trusted Friends and Family: Share your journey with trusted friends and family members who offer encouragement and support. Open communication fosters understanding and validation.

8. Practicing Emotional Regulation:

EMOTIONAL REGULATION involves managing and expressing your emotions in healthy ways.

Techniques for Emotional Regulation:

1. DEEP BREATHING: Practice deep breathing exercises to stay calm and centered.

2. Mindfulness: Use mindfulness techniques to stay present and observe your emotions without judgment.

3. Journaling: Write about your emotions and experiences to process and understand them.

4. Healthy Outlets: Find healthy outlets for your emotions, such as exercise, creative expression, or talking to a trusted friend.

Building Independence and Healthy Interdependence

BUILDING INDEPENDENCE and healthy interdependence involves balancing self-sufficiency with the ability to form mutually supportive and respectful relationships. It requires cultivating a sense of autonomy while also recognizing the value of connection and collaboration.

1. Understanding Healthy Interdependence:

HEALTHY INTERDEPENDENCE is a relationship dynamic where both individuals maintain their independence while also supporting and relying on each other. It involves mutual respect, trust, and equality.

Characteristics of Healthy Interdependence:

- MUTUAL SUPPORT: BOTH individuals provide emotional and practical support to each other.

- Respect for Boundaries: Boundaries are respected and honored by both parties.

- Equality: The relationship is balanced, with both individuals contributing and receiving equally.

- Emotional Intimacy: There is a deep sense of emotional intimacy and connection based on trust and respect.

- Independence: Both individuals maintain their independence and pursue their interests and goals.

2. Cultivating Self-Respect and Self-Worth:

CULTIVATING SELF-RESPECT and self-worth is essential for building healthy interdependence. It involves recognizing your intrinsic value and treating yourself with dignity and respect.

Steps for Cultivating Self-Respect and Self-Worth:

1. SELF-COMPASSION: Practice self-compassion by treating yourself with kindness and understanding.

2. Affirmations: Use positive affirmations to reinforce your self-worth.

3. Celebrate Achievements: Acknowledge and celebrate your achievements and successes.

4. Self-Care: Engage in self-care activities that nurture your well-being.

3. Developing Healthy Relationship Skills:

DEVELOPING HEALTHY relationship skills involves learning to communicate effectively, set boundaries, and build trust.

Steps for Developing Healthy Relationship Skills:

1. EFFECTIVE COMMUNICATION: Practice active listening and use "I" statements to express your feelings and needs.

2. Setting Boundaries: Set and maintain healthy boundaries to protect your well-being.

3. Building Trust: Build trust by being reliable, honest, and respectful.

4. Emotional Intimacy: Foster emotional intimacy by sharing your thoughts and feelings openly and honestly.

4. Balancing Independence and Connection:

BALANCING INDEPENDENCE and connection involves maintaining your sense of self while also nurturing your relationships.

Steps for Balancing Independence and Connection:

1. PURSUE PERSONAL Interests: Engage in activities and hobbies that bring you joy and fulfillment.

2. Set Personal Goals: Set personal goals and work towards achieving them.

3. Spend Time Alone: Spend time alone to reflect, recharge, and connect with yourself.

4. **Nurture Relationships:** Nurture your relationships by spending quality time with loved ones and providing support and understanding.

5. Embracing Vulnerability:

EMBRACING VULNERABILITY involves being open and honest about your feelings and experiences. It fosters deeper connections and mutual understanding.

Steps for Embracing Vulnerability:

1. SHARE YOUR FEELINGS: Share your thoughts and feelings with trusted individuals.

2. Seek Support: Seek support from others when needed.

3. Be Open to Feedback: Be open to receiving feedback and constructive criticism.

4. Practice Self-Compassion: Treat yourself with kindness and understanding when feeling vulnerable.

6. Fostering Mutual Respect:

MUTUAL RESPECT IS THE foundation of healthy interdependence. It involves valuing and honoring each other's needs, boundaries, and individuality.

Steps for Fostering Mutual Respect:

1. RESPECT BOUNDARIES: Respect and honor each other's boundaries.

2. Communicate Openly: Communicate openly and honestly about your needs and feelings.

3. Support Each Other: Provide emotional and practical support to each other.

4. Celebrate Individuality: Celebrate and appreciate each other's uniqueness and individuality.

7. Building a Support Network:

BUILDING A SUPPORT network involves connecting with individuals who understand and support your journey.

Steps for Building a Support Network:

1. ENGAGE WITH MULTIPLE Sources: Utilize a combination of therapy, support groups, and personal relationships to create a comprehensive support network.

2. Communicate Openly: Share your experiences and needs with trusted individuals in your network.

3. Participate Actively: Engage actively in therapy and support groups to maximize the benefits.

4. Seek Ongoing Support: Continuously seek out and engage with resources that align with your changing needs.

8. Embracing Personal Growth:

EMBRACING PERSONAL growth involves continuously learning and developing new skills and insights.

Steps for Embracing Personal Growth:

1. SET GROWTH GOALS: Identify areas of your life where you want to grow and improve.

2. Seek Learning Opportunities: Seek out opportunities for learning and development, such as courses, workshops, or books.

3. Reflect on Progress: Reflect on your progress and celebrate your achievements.

4. Stay Open to New Experiences: Stay open to new experiences and be willing to step outside your comfort zone.

Conclusion

Overcoming codependency is a journey of self-discovery, healing, and growth. Understanding codependency and its signs, breaking free from codependent behaviors, and building independence and healthy interdependence are essential steps in this process. By implementing the techniques and strategies outlined in this chapter, you can develop a strong sense of self-worth, cultivate healthy relationships, and create a fulfilling and empowered life.

Remember that overcoming codependency takes time and effort. Be patient and compassionate with yourself as you navigate this journey. Seek support when needed, prioritize your well-being, and celebrate your progress and growth. By taking these steps, you can break free from codependent patterns and move toward a life of resilience, empowerment, and healthy interdependence.

As you continue reading this book, you will find additional insights, strategies, and encouragement to support your healing journey. Each chapter provides practical tools and inspiring stories to help you navigate the complexities of your experiences and move toward a life of resilience and empowerment.

Chapter 11: Establishing Financial Independence

Financial Challenges Faced by Adult Children of Substance Abusers

Growing up in a household affected by substance abuse presents unique financial challenges. These challenges can hinder the development of healthy financial habits and impede the path to financial independence. Understanding these obstacles is the first step toward overcoming them and achieving financial stability.

1. Financial Instability in the Household:

HOUSEHOLDS WITH SUBSTANCE-abusing parents often experience significant financial instability. Funds that should be allocated for essential needs such as housing, food, and education may be diverted to support the addiction. This misallocation of resources can result in chronic financial stress and uncertainty for the entire family.

2. Lack of Financial Education:

CHILDREN IN THESE ENVIRONMENTS frequently receive inadequate financial education. Substance-abusing parents may be unable to model responsible financial behavior or provide guidance on budgeting, saving, and investing. As a result, adult children of substance abusers may enter adulthood with limited financial literacy and an understanding of money management.

3. Debt and Financial Obligations:

MANY ADULT CHILDREN of substance abusers inherit debt or financial obligations from their parents. They may be pressured to contribute financially to the household from a young age or assume responsibility for unpaid bills and debts. This added financial burden can delay their ability to achieve financial independence.

4. Emotional Spending and Financial Avoidance:

GROWING UP IN A STRESSFUL and unstable environment can lead to emotional spending and financial avoidance as coping mechanisms. Adult children of substance abusers may use spending as a way to manage stress and emotions or avoid dealing with financial responsibilities altogether. These behaviors can contribute to financial instability and debt.

5. Limited Access to Resources:

ACCESS TO RESOURCES such as higher education, stable employment, and financial support systems may be limited for adult children of substance abusers. The chaotic and unpredictable nature of their upbringing can interfere with academic and career development, limiting opportunities for financial advancement.

6. Codependency and Financial Enabling:

CODEPENDENCY OFTEN extends to financial behaviors. Adult children of substance abusers may feel compelled to financially support their parents or siblings, even at the expense of their own financial well-being. This enabling behavior can perpetuate financial instability and hinder the path to independence.

7. Mental Health and Financial Stress:

THE EMOTIONAL AND PSYCHOLOGICAL toll of growing up with a substance-abusing parent can impact mental health, leading to issues such as anxiety, depression, and PTSD. These mental health challenges can further complicate financial management and decision-making, creating a cycle of financial stress and instability.

Strategies for Achieving Financial Stability

ACHIEVING FINANCIAL stability requires a combination of practical financial strategies, emotional resilience, and a commitment to long-term goals. Here are several strategies to help adult children of substance abusers build a stable financial foundation.

1. Developing Financial Literacy:

BUILDING FINANCIAL literacy is essential for managing money effectively and making informed financial decisions.

Steps for Developing Financial Literacy:

1. EDUCATE YOURSELF: Take advantage of financial education resources such as books, online courses, and workshops. Learn about budgeting, saving, investing, and debt management.

2. Seek Professional Advice: Consult with financial advisors or counselors to gain personalized guidance and support. They can help you develop a financial plan and address specific challenges.

3. Join Financial Literacy Programs: Participate in financial literacy programs offered by community organizations, banks, or educational institutions. These programs often provide practical tools and resources for managing money.

2. Creating a Budget:

A BUDGET IS A CRUCIAL tool for tracking income and expenses, setting financial goals, and ensuring that you live within your means.

Steps for Creating a Budget:

1. TRACK INCOME AND Expenses: Record all sources of income and track your expenses for a month to understand your spending patterns.

2. Categorize Expenses: Divide your expenses into categories such as housing, utilities, groceries, transportation, entertainment, and savings.

3. Set Spending Limits: Allocate a specific amount of money to each category based on your income and financial goals. Ensure that your total expenses do not exceed your income.

4. Monitor and Adjust: Regularly review and adjust your budget to reflect changes in income, expenses, or financial goals.

3. Building an Emergency Fund:

AN EMERGENCY FUND PROVIDES financial security and peace of mind by covering unexpected expenses such as medical bills, car repairs, or job loss.

Steps for Building an Emergency Fund:

1. SET A SAVINGS GOAL: Aim to save three to six months' worth of living expenses in your emergency fund.

2. Start Small: Begin by setting aside a small amount each month, even if it's just $20 or $50. Consistency is key.

3. Automate Savings: Set up automatic transfers to a separate savings account dedicated to your emergency fund.

4. Prioritize Savings: Treat your emergency fund contributions as a non-negotiable expense in your budget.

4. Managing and Reducing Debt:

MANAGING AND REDUCING debt is essential for achieving financial stability and independence.

Steps for Managing and Reducing Debt:

1. LIST YOUR DEBTS: Create a list of all your debts, including credit cards, student loans, personal loans, and any other obligations. Include the interest rates and minimum payments for each.

2. Prioritize High-Interest Debt: Focus on paying off high-interest debt first, as it accumulates the most interest over time.

3. Create a Repayment Plan: Develop a repayment plan that includes making at least the minimum payments on all debts while allocating extra funds to the highest-interest debt.

4. Consider Debt Consolidation: Explore options for consolidating debt, such as balance transfer credit cards or personal loans, to simplify payments and reduce interest rates.

5. Avoid New Debt: Limit the use of credit cards and avoid taking on new debt while working to pay off existing obligations.

5. Saving and Investing:

SAVING AND INVESTING are crucial for building wealth and achieving long-term financial goals.

Steps for Saving and Investing:

1. SET FINANCIAL GOALS: Identify short-term and long-term financial goals, such as saving for a vacation, buying a home, or retirement.

2. Open Savings Accounts: Open separate savings accounts for different goals to keep your savings organized and track progress.

3. Start Investing: Begin investing in retirement accounts, such as a 401(k) or IRA, and explore other investment options like stocks, bonds, and mutual funds. Consider consulting a financial advisor for guidance.

4. Diversify Investments: Diversify your investments to spread risk and increase potential returns. Avoid putting all your money into a single investment.

6. Establishing Good Credit:

A GOOD CREDIT SCORE is essential for accessing favorable loan terms, renting apartments, and even securing certain jobs.

Steps for Establishing Good Credit:

1. CHECK YOUR CREDIT Report: Obtain a free copy of your credit report from each of the three major credit bureaus (Equifax, Experian, and TransUnion) and review it for accuracy.

2. Pay Bills on Time: Ensure that all bills, including credit card payments, loans, and utilities, are paid on time. Set up automatic payments or reminders if needed.

3. Keep Balances Low: Aim to keep your credit card balances below 30% of your credit limit to maintain a healthy credit utilization ratio.

4. Build a Credit History: If you have limited or no credit history, consider applying for a secured credit card or becoming an authorized user on someone else's credit card to build credit.

7. Seeking Support and Resources:

SEEKING SUPPORT AND utilizing available resources can provide valuable guidance and assistance in achieving financial stability.

Sources of Support and Resources:

1. FINANCIAL COUNSELORS: Financial counselors can provide personalized advice and support for managing money, reducing debt, and achieving financial goals.

2. Community Organizations: Many community organizations offer financial literacy programs, workshops, and resources to help individuals improve their financial health.

3. Online Tools and Apps: Utilize online tools and apps for budgeting, saving, and tracking expenses. Many apps offer features like goal setting, automatic savings, and spending analysis.

4. Support Groups:*

Join support groups or online communities focused on financial wellness. Sharing experiences and learning from others can provide motivation and practical tips.

8. Building a Strong Financial Mindset:

DEVELOPING A STRONG financial mindset involves cultivating healthy attitudes and behaviors toward money.

Steps for Building a Strong Financial Mindset:

1. SET INTENTIONS: Set clear intentions for your financial future and commit to making positive changes.

2. Practice Gratitude: Practice gratitude for what you have and focus on the positive aspects of your financial journey.

3. Stay Positive: Maintain a positive outlook and believe in your ability to achieve financial stability and independence.

4. Learn from Mistakes: View financial mistakes as learning opportunities and use them to make better decisions in the future.

Planning for a Secure Financial Future

PLANNING FOR A SECURE financial future involves setting long-term goals, creating a comprehensive financial plan, and taking proactive steps to ensure financial security and growth.

1. Setting Long-Term Financial Goals:

LONG-TERM FINANCIAL goals provide direction and motivation for your financial journey. These goals can include saving for retirement, buying a home, or funding your children's education.

Steps for Setting Long-Term Financial Goals:

1. IDENTIFY GOALS: Identify specific, measurable, achievable, relevant, and time-bound (SMART) financial goals.

2. Prioritize Goals: Prioritize your goals based on their importance and timeline. Focus on achieving the most critical goals first.

3. Break Down Goals: Break down long-term goals into smaller, manageable milestones to track progress and stay motivated.

4. Review and Adjust: Regularly review and adjust your goals as needed to reflect changes in your financial situation or priorities.

2. Creating a Comprehensive Financial Plan:

A COMPREHENSIVE FINANCIAL plan outlines the steps and strategies needed to achieve your long-term financial goals.

Steps for Creating a Financial Plan:

1. ASSESS YOUR CURRENT Situation: Evaluate your current financial situation, including income, expenses, assets, liabilities, and net worth.

2. Define Goals: Clearly define your short-term and long-term financial goals.

3. Develop a Budget: Create a budget that aligns with your goals and ensures that you live within your means.

4. Build an Emergency Fund: Prioritize building an emergency fund to cover unexpected expenses.

5. Reduce Debt: Develop a plan to manage and reduce debt.

6. Save and Invest: Establish a savings and investment strategy to build wealth and achieve long-term goals.

7. Plan for Retirement: Plan for retirement by contributing to retirement accounts and exploring additional investment options.

8. Review and Adjust: Regularly review and adjust your financial plan to reflect changes in your financial situation or goals.

3. Planning for Retirement:

PLANNING FOR RETIREMENT is a critical component of long-term financial security. It involves saving and investing to ensure a comfortable and financially secure retirement.

Steps for Planning for Retirement:

1. SET RETIREMENT GOALS: Determine your retirement goals, including your desired retirement age, lifestyle, and financial needs.

2. Estimate Retirement Expenses: Estimate your retirement expenses based on your goals and current lifestyle. Consider factors such as housing, healthcare, travel, and leisure activities.

3. Contribute to Retirement Accounts: Contribute regularly to retirement accounts such as a 401(k), IRA, or Roth IRA. Take advantage of employer matching contributions if available.

4. Diversify Investments: Diversify your retirement investments to spread risk and increase potential returns. Consider a mix of stocks, bonds, and other investment options.

5. Monitor and Adjust: Regularly review and adjust your retirement plan to ensure that you stay on track to meet your goals.

4. Protecting Your Assets:

PROTECTING YOUR ASSETS involves implementing strategies to safeguard your financial resources and ensure long-term security.

Steps for Protecting Your Assets:

1. INSURANCE COVERAGE: Obtain adequate insurance coverage, including health, life, disability, and property insurance. Ensure that your coverage aligns with your needs and financial goals.

2. Estate Planning: Create an estate plan that includes a will, power of attorney, and healthcare directive. Consider establishing a trust to manage and protect your assets.

3. Legal Protections: Consult with a financial advisor or attorney to explore additional legal protections, such as prenuptial agreements or business structures.

4. Emergency Fund: Maintain an emergency fund to cover unexpected expenses and protect your assets from financial setbacks.

5. Planning for Major Life Events:

PLANNING FOR MAJOR life events, such as buying a home, starting a family, or pursuing higher education, involves careful financial planning and preparation.

Steps for Planning for Major Life Events:

1. SET CLEAR GOALS: Define your goals for major life events and determine the associated costs.

2. Save and Budget: Create a savings plan and budget to allocate funds for these events.

3. Research and Plan: Research the financial aspects of your goals, such as mortgage options, education expenses, or childcare costs. Develop a detailed plan to achieve these goals.

4. Seek Professional Advice: Consult with financial advisors or experts to gain insights and guidance on planning for major life events.

6. Building Wealth and Generational Financial Security:

BUILDING WEALTH AND ensuring generational financial security involves creating a legacy of financial stability and prosperity for future generations.

Steps for Building Wealth and Generational Financial Security:

1. INVEST WISELY: DEVELOP a diversified investment strategy to build wealth over time. Consider long-term investments that align with your financial goals.

2. Financial Education: Educate yourself and your family about financial literacy and money management. Foster a culture of financial responsibility and empowerment.

3. Estate Planning: Create an estate plan to transfer wealth to future generations. Consider setting up trusts, gifting strategies, or other mechanisms to manage and protect your assets.

4. Philanthropy: Consider philanthropic efforts, such as charitable donations or establishing a family foundation, to leave a positive legacy and support causes that are important to you.

7. Staying Informed and Adaptable:

STAYING INFORMED AND adaptable is essential for navigating the ever-changing financial landscape and ensuring long-term financial success.

Steps for Staying Informed and Adaptable:

1. CONTINUOUS LEARNING: Stay informed about financial trends, market conditions, and new investment opportunities. Engage in continuous learning through books, courses, and financial news.

2. Seek Professional Advice: Regularly consult with financial advisors or experts to gain insights and make informed decisions.

3. Review and Adjust: Regularly review your financial plan, goals, and investments. Be adaptable and willing to make adjustments as needed to stay on track.

4. Stay Resilient: Maintain a positive and resilient mindset, recognizing that financial setbacks and challenges are part of the journey. Stay focused on your long-term goals and continue to take proactive steps toward financial security.

Conclusion

Establishing financial independence is a multifaceted journey that involves overcoming unique challenges, implementing practical strategies, and planning for a secure financial future. By understanding the financial challenges faced by adult children of substance abusers, developing financial literacy, creating a budget, building an emergency fund, managing and reducing debt, saving and investing, establishing good credit, seeking support, and cultivating a strong financial mindset, you can achieve financial stability and independence.

Planning for a secure financial future requires setting long-term goals, creating a comprehensive financial plan, planning for retirement, protecting your assets, preparing for major life events, building wealth, and staying informed and adaptable. By taking these proactive steps, you can create a foundation of financial security and prosperity for yourself and future generations.

Remember that achieving financial independence takes time, effort, and perseverance. Be patient and compassionate with yourself as you navigate this journey. Seek support when needed, prioritize your financial well-being, and celebrate your progress and achievements. By taking these steps, you can move toward a life of financial stability, independence, and empowerment.

As you continue reading this book, you will find additional insights, strategies, and encouragement to support your healing journey. Each chapter provides practical tools and inspiring stories to help you navigate the complexities of your experiences and move toward a life of resilience and empowerment.

Chapter 12: Building a Support Network

Importance of a Strong Support System

A strong support system is crucial for anyone striving for personal growth, healing, and resilience, especially for adult children of substance abusers. A supportive network provides emotional, psychological, and practical assistance that can help mitigate the challenges associated with overcoming past trauma and navigating the complexities of adult life.

1. Emotional Support:

EMOTIONAL SUPPORT IS fundamental in coping with the stress, anxiety, and emotional turmoil often experienced by adult children of substance abusers. Supportive relationships offer a safe space to express feelings, share experiences, and receive empathy and understanding.

2. Psychological Well-Being:

A ROBUST SUPPORT NETWORK positively impacts psychological well-being. It helps individuals feel valued, understood, and connected, reducing feelings of isolation and loneliness. This sense of belonging is essential for maintaining mental health and fostering a positive self-image.

3. Practical Assistance:

SUPPORT SYSTEMS CAN provide practical assistance, such as helping with daily tasks, offering financial support, or providing guidance in decision-making. This practical help can alleviate stress and enable individuals to focus on personal growth and healing.

4. Encouragement and Motivation:

A STRONG SUPPORT NETWORK offers encouragement and motivation to pursue goals, overcome challenges, and persist through difficult times. Supportive relationships provide a source of inspiration and accountability, helping individuals stay committed to their personal and professional aspirations.

5. Resilience Building:

SUPPORT SYSTEMS PLAY a crucial role in building resilience. They provide a foundation of stability and security, enabling individuals to bounce back from setbacks and adversity. Resilience is essential for navigating the complexities of life and maintaining a positive outlook.

6. Validation and Acceptance:

SUPPORTIVE RELATIONSHIPS offer validation and acceptance, helping individuals feel acknowledged and valued. This validation is particularly important for those who may have experienced invalidation or neglect in their upbringing.

7. Stress Reduction:

A STRONG SUPPORT SYSTEM can significantly reduce stress by providing emotional and practical support. Knowing that there are people to turn to in times of need can alleviate anxiety and foster a sense of security.

8. Health Benefits:

NUMEROUS STUDIES HAVE shown that strong social connections contribute to better physical health outcomes. Supportive relationships are associated with lower rates of depression, anxiety, and chronic illnesses, as well as improved immune function and longevity.

How to Seek and Cultivate Supportive Relationships

SEEKING AND CULTIVATING supportive relationships involves intentional efforts to connect with others, build trust, and maintain healthy interactions. Here are strategies to develop and nurture a strong support network:

1. Identifying Potential Supportive Relationships:

START BY IDENTIFYING individuals in your life who have the potential to be supportive. These may include family members, friends, colleagues, mentors, or members of your community.

Steps for Identifying Potential Supportive Relationships:

1. REFLECT ON EXISTING Relationships: Reflect on your current relationships and identify those who have been supportive or have the potential to be.

2. Assess Compatibility: Consider the compatibility of your values, interests, and goals with those of potential supporters. Look for individuals who share common ground and mutual respect.

3. Seek Positive Influences: Focus on relationships that have a positive influence on your well-being and growth. Avoid toxic or draining relationships that hinder your progress.

2. Building Trust and Connection:

BUILDING TRUST AND connection is essential for developing supportive relationships. Trust is the foundation of any healthy relationship and fosters open communication and mutual understanding.

Steps for Building Trust and Connection:

1. BE AUTHENTIC: BE genuine and authentic in your interactions. Share your thoughts, feelings, and experiences honestly and openly.

2. Show Empathy: Practice empathy by actively listening to others and showing understanding and compassion for their experiences.

3. Communicate Effectively: Use effective communication techniques, such as active listening, "I" statements, and nonverbal cues, to foster understanding and connection.

4. Be Reliable: Follow through on commitments and be dependable. Consistency and reliability build trust over time.

5. Respect Boundaries: Respect others' boundaries and communicate your own. Healthy boundaries are essential for maintaining trust and mutual respect.

3. Nurturing Relationships:

NURTURING RELATIONSHIPS involves ongoing efforts to maintain and strengthen connections. Invest time and energy in your relationships to ensure they remain supportive and fulfilling.

Steps for Nurturing Relationships:

1. SPEND QUALITY TIME: Spend quality time with supportive individuals, engaging in activities you both enjoy. Regularly check in and stay connected.

2. Offer Support: Offer emotional and practical support to others in your network. Reciprocity strengthens relationships and fosters a sense of mutual care.

3. Express Appreciation: Show appreciation and gratitude for the support you receive. Expressing gratitude reinforces positive behaviors and deepens connections.

4. Resolve Conflicts: Address conflicts and misunderstandings promptly and constructively. Use effective conflict resolution techniques to maintain healthy relationships.

4. Expanding Your Support Network:

EXPANDING YOUR SUPPORT network involves seeking new connections and diversifying your sources of support. A diverse network provides a broader range of perspectives and resources.

Steps for Expanding Your Support Network:

1. JOIN GROUPS AND Organizations: Join groups, clubs, or organizations that align with your interests and values. These settings provide opportunities to meet like-minded individuals.

2. Attend Social Events: Attend social events, workshops, and community gatherings to expand your social circle and build new connections.

3. Seek Mentors: Identify mentors who can offer guidance, support, and wisdom. Mentors can provide valuable insights and help you navigate challenges.

4. Utilize Online Communities: Engage with online communities and support groups. Online platforms offer opportunities to connect with individuals who share similar experiences and goals.

5. Maintaining Healthy Boundaries:

MAINTAINING HEALTHY boundaries is crucial for ensuring that your support network remains positive and beneficial. Boundaries protect your well-being and foster respectful interactions.

Steps for Maintaining Healthy Boundaries:

1. IDENTIFY YOUR BOUNDARIES: Reflect on your needs, limits, and values to identify your boundaries in relationships.

2. Communicate Boundaries: Clearly communicate your boundaries to others and explain their importance.

3. Enforce Boundaries: Consistently enforce your boundaries and follow through with consequences if they are violated.

4. Respect Others' Boundaries: Respect and honor the boundaries of others. Mutual respect is essential for maintaining healthy relationships.

Leveraging Community Resources

COMMUNITY RESOURCES offer valuable support, information, and services that can enhance your well-being and facilitate personal growth. Leveraging these resources involves identifying and accessing the support available in your community.

1. Identifying Community Resources:

START BY IDENTIFYING the community resources available to you. These resources may include social services, support groups, educational programs, and recreational facilities.

Steps for Identifying Community Resources:

1. RESEARCH LOCAL ORGANIZATIONS: Research local organizations, nonprofits, and government agencies that offer services and support. Look for organizations that align with your needs and interests.

2. Ask for Recommendations: Seek recommendations from friends, family, healthcare providers, or community members. Personal referrals can provide valuable insights into available resources.

3. Utilize Online Directories: Use online directories and databases to search for community resources. Websites such as 211.org provide information on local services and support.

2. Accessing Social Services:

SOCIAL SERVICES OFFER a range of support, including financial assistance, healthcare, housing, and mental health services. Accessing these services can provide essential support during times of need.

Steps for Accessing Social Services:

1. IDENTIFY YOUR NEEDS: Identify your specific needs, such as financial assistance, healthcare, housing, or mental health support.

2. Contact Agencies: Contact relevant agencies or organizations to inquire about available services and eligibility criteria.

3. Complete Applications: Complete any required applications or documentation to access services. Provide accurate and detailed information to facilitate the process.

4. Follow Up: Follow up with agencies to ensure your application is processed and to stay informed about the status of your request.

3. Participating in Support Groups:

SUPPORT GROUPS OFFER a sense of community and shared experience, providing valuable emotional support and practical advice.

Types of Support Groups:

1. PEER SUPPORT GROUPS: Peer-led groups consist of individuals with similar experiences who come together to share stories, provide support, and offer practical advice. These groups foster a sense of camaraderie and mutual understanding.

2. Therapist-Led Groups: These groups are facilitated by a licensed therapist and offer a combination of support and therapeutic intervention. They often focus on specific issues, such as trauma, anxiety, or relationship dynamics.

3. 12-Step Programs: Programs such as Al-Anon and Adult Children of Alcoholics (ACA) follow a structured, 12-step approach to recovery and support. These groups provide a framework for addressing the impact of a parent's addiction and fostering personal growth.

Steps for Participating in Support Groups:

1. IDENTIFY SUITABLE Groups: Identify support groups that align with your needs and experiences. Consider factors such as the group's focus, format (in-person or virtual), and meeting frequency.

2. Attend Meetings: Attend a few meetings to assess the group's dynamics, structure, and whether it meets your needs. Pay attention to how comfortable you feel and whether the group provides the support you are seeking.

3. Engage Actively: Engage actively in the group by sharing your experiences, offering support to others, and participating in discussions. Active participation enhances the benefits of the group.

4. Build Relationships: Build relationships with group members outside of meetings. Forming connections and maintaining contact can provide additional support and foster a sense of community.

4. Utilizing Educational Programs:

EDUCATIONAL PROGRAMS offer opportunities for personal and professional growth, providing valuable knowledge and skills.

Types of Educational Programs:

1. WORKSHOPS AND SEMINARS: Attend workshops and seminars on topics of interest, such as financial literacy, mental health, career development, or personal growth.

2. Community Classes: Enroll in community classes or adult education programs to learn new skills or pursue hobbies.

3. Online Courses: Take advantage of online courses and webinars to gain knowledge and skills from the comfort of your home.

4. Mentorship Programs: Participate in mentorship programs that connect you with experienced individuals who can offer guidance and support.

Steps for Utilizing Educational Programs:

1. IDENTIFY YOUR INTERESTS: Identify your interests and goals to determine the types of educational programs that align with your aspirations.

2. Research Options: Research available programs, considering factors such as location, format, cost, and content.

3. Enroll and Participate: Enroll in programs that meet your needs and actively participate in classes and activities. Take advantage of networking opportunities and resources provided.

4. Apply Learnings: Apply the knowledge and skills gained from educational programs to your personal and professional life. Continuously seek opportunities for growth and development.

5. Engaging with Recreational Facilities:

RECREATIONAL FACILITIES offer opportunities for physical activity, social interaction, and relaxation, contributing to overall well-being.

Types of Recreational Facilities:

1. COMMUNITY CENTERS: Community centers often provide fitness classes, recreational activities, and social events.

2. Parks and Recreation: Local parks and recreation departments offer outdoor activities, sports leagues, and nature programs.

3. Fitness Centers: Join fitness centers or gyms to participate in exercise classes, use fitness equipment, and engage in physical activities.

4. Cultural Institutions: Explore cultural institutions such as museums, theaters, and art galleries for educational and recreational experiences.

Steps for Engaging with Recreational Facilities:

1. IDENTIFY ACTIVITIES: Identify activities and interests that bring you joy and fulfillment.

2. Research Facilities: Research local recreational facilities and programs that offer these activities.

3. Join and Participate: Join facilities or programs that align with your interests and actively participate in activities. Engage with others and build social connections.

4. Explore New Interests: Be open to exploring new activities and interests to diversify your recreational experiences.

6. Volunteering and Giving Back:

VOLUNTEERING AND GIVING back to the community provide a sense of purpose, fulfillment, and connection. It also offers opportunities to build new relationships and develop skills.

Benefits of Volunteering:

1. SOCIAL CONNECTION: Volunteering provides opportunities to meet new people and build social connections.

2. Personal Growth: Volunteering fosters personal growth, empathy, and a sense of accomplishment.

3. Skill Development: Volunteering allows you to develop new skills and gain valuable experience.

4. Community Impact: Volunteering contributes to the well-being of the community and supports important causes.

Steps for Volunteering:

1. IDENTIFY CAUSES: Identify causes and organizations that align with your values and interests.

2. Research Opportunities: Research volunteer opportunities in your community or online. Consider factors such as time commitment, location, and type of work.

3. Apply and Commit: Apply for volunteer positions and commit to regular participation. Treat volunteering as a meaningful and important responsibility.

4. Engage and Reflect: Engage fully in your volunteer work and reflect on the impact it has on you and the community. Use the experience to grow and build connections.

Conclusion

Building a strong support network is essential for personal growth, healing, and resilience, especially for adult children of substance abusers. A supportive network provides emotional, psychological, and practical assistance, helping individuals navigate challenges and achieve their goals. By seeking and cultivating supportive relationships, leveraging community resources, and maintaining healthy boundaries, you can develop a robust support system that enhances your well-being and fosters a sense of belonging.

Remember that building a support network takes time and effort. Be patient and intentional in your efforts to connect with others and maintain supportive relationships. Seek out community resources, participate in support groups, engage in educational programs, and take advantage of recreational facilities to enhance your support system. Volunteering and giving back to the community also provide opportunities for connection, growth, and fulfillment.

As you continue reading this book, you will find additional insights, strategies, and encouragement to support your healing journey. Each chapter provides practical tools and inspiring stories to help you navigate the complexities of your experiences and move toward a life of resilience and empowerment.

Chapter 13: Creating a Healthy Lifestyle

Importance of Physical Health and Wellness

Physical health and wellness are fundamental aspects of a healthy lifestyle, impacting both mental and emotional well-being. For adult children of substance abusers, focusing on physical health can provide stability, resilience, and a sense of control amidst the complexities of their upbringing. Here's why physical health and wellness are crucial:

1. Enhancing Mental Health:

REGULAR PHYSICAL ACTIVITY and a balanced diet contribute significantly to mental health. Exercise releases endorphins, which are natural mood lifters, and reduces symptoms of anxiety and depression. Good nutrition supports brain function, energy levels, and overall mood stability.

2. Building Resilience:

PHYSICAL HEALTH FOSTERS resilience by enhancing the body's ability to cope with stress and recover from illnesses. Regular exercise, adequate sleep, and a nutritious diet strengthen the immune system and improve overall vitality.

3. Promoting Emotional Stability:

PHYSICAL WELL-BEING is closely linked to emotional stability. Exercise and proper nutrition help regulate mood, reduce stress, and promote a sense of well-being. Engaging in physical activities can also serve as a healthy outlet for managing emotions.

4. Increasing Energy Levels:

A HEALTHY LIFESTYLE increases energy levels, enabling individuals to be more productive and engaged in their daily activities. Regular exercise improves cardiovascular health and stamina, while balanced nutrition ensures the body receives the essential nutrients it needs.

5. Improving Sleep Quality:

QUALITY SLEEP IS CRUCIAL for overall health. Regular physical activity and a balanced diet can improve sleep patterns, leading to better rest and rejuvenation. Good sleep hygiene practices further enhance sleep quality and contribute to overall well-being.

6. Enhancing Cognitive Function:

PHYSICAL HEALTH POSITIVELY impacts cognitive function, including memory, concentration, and decision-making abilities. Regular exercise promotes neuroplasticity, the brain's ability to adapt and grow, while proper nutrition supports cognitive health.

7. Preventing Chronic Diseases:

A HEALTHY LIFESTYLE helps prevent chronic diseases such as heart disease, diabetes, obesity, and certain cancers. Regular physical activity, a balanced diet, and avoiding harmful habits like smoking and excessive drinking contribute to long-term health.

8. Boosting Self-Esteem and Confidence:

ENGAGING IN REGULAR physical activity and maintaining a healthy lifestyle can boost self-esteem and confidence. Achieving fitness goals, feeling strong and healthy, and taking care of oneself contribute to a positive self-image.

Developing a Balanced Lifestyle

DEVELOPING A BALANCED lifestyle involves integrating various aspects of physical, mental, and emotional health into daily routines. It requires intentional efforts to create harmony between work, personal life, and self-care. Here are key components and strategies for developing a balanced lifestyle:

1. Prioritizing Physical Activity:

REGULAR PHYSICAL ACTIVITY is essential for overall health and well-being. It helps manage weight, reduce the risk of chronic diseases, improve mental health, and enhance quality of life.

Steps for Prioritizing Physical Activity:

1. SET REALISTIC GOALS: Set achievable fitness goals based on your current fitness level and personal preferences. Start with small, manageable steps and gradually increase intensity and duration.

2. Choose Activities You Enjoy: Engage in physical activities that you enjoy, whether it's walking, running, cycling, swimming, dancing, or playing a sport. Enjoyable activities are more likely to become regular habits.

3. Create a Routine: Establish a regular exercise routine by scheduling specific times for physical activity. Consistency is key to making exercise a habit.

4. Incorporate Variety: Incorporate a variety of activities to keep your routine interesting and well-rounded. Include cardio, strength training, flexibility exercises, and relaxation practices.

5. Stay Active Throughout the Day: Look for opportunities to stay active throughout the day, such as taking the stairs, walking or biking to work, or doing short workouts during breaks.

2. Eating a Balanced Diet:

A BALANCED DIET PROVIDES the essential nutrients needed for optimal health. It supports physical and mental well-being, energy levels, and disease prevention.

Steps for Eating a Balanced Diet:

1. FOCUS ON WHOLE FOODS: Emphasize whole, unprocessed foods such as fruits, vegetables, whole grains, lean proteins, and healthy fats. These foods provide essential nutrients and are less likely to contain added sugars and unhealthy fats.

2. Portion Control: Pay attention to portion sizes to avoid overeating. Use smaller plates, eat slowly, and listen to your body's hunger and fullness cues.

3. Stay Hydrated: Drink plenty of water throughout the day to stay hydrated. Water is essential for digestion, circulation, temperature regulation, and overall health.

4. Limit Processed Foods: Reduce the consumption of processed foods, sugary snacks, and beverages. These foods often contain unhealthy additives and lack essential nutrients.

5. Plan and Prepare Meals: Plan and prepare balanced meals and snacks ahead of time to ensure you have healthy options available. Meal planning helps avoid impulsive and unhealthy food choices.

3. Ensuring Adequate Sleep:

QUALITY SLEEP IS VITAL for physical, mental, and emotional health. It supports cognitive function, mood regulation, and overall well-being.

Steps for Ensuring Adequate Sleep:

1. ESTABLISH A SLEEP Routine: Create a consistent sleep routine by going to bed and waking up at the same time every day, even on weekends.

2. Create a Sleep-Friendly Environment: Make your bedroom conducive to sleep by keeping it cool, dark, and quiet. Use comfortable bedding and minimize disruptions.

3. Limit Screen Time: Avoid screens (phones, tablets, computers, TV) at least an hour before bedtime. The blue light emitted by screens can interfere with the production of melatonin, the hormone that regulates sleep.

4. Avoid Stimulants: Avoid caffeine, nicotine, and heavy meals close to bedtime, as they can disrupt sleep.

5. Relax Before Bed: Develop a relaxing pre-sleep routine, such as reading, taking a warm bath, or practicing relaxation techniques like deep breathing or meditation.

4. Managing Stress:

EFFECTIVE STRESS MANAGEMENT is crucial for maintaining a balanced lifestyle. Chronic stress can negatively impact physical and mental health.

Steps for Managing Stress:

1. IDENTIFY STRESSORS: Identify the sources of stress in your life and evaluate how they affect you. Understanding your stressors can help you develop strategies to manage them.

2. Practice Relaxation Techniques: Incorporate relaxation techniques such as deep breathing, progressive muscle relaxation, meditation, and yoga into your daily routine to reduce stress.

3. Stay Organized: Keep a well-organized schedule to manage your time effectively and reduce feelings of overwhelm. Prioritize tasks and break them into manageable steps.

4. Set Boundaries: Set healthy boundaries to protect your time and energy. Learn to say no to commitments that add unnecessary stress.

5. Seek Support: Reach out to friends, family, or a therapist for support and guidance. Talking about your stressors can provide relief and new perspectives.

5. Cultivating Healthy Relationships:

HEALTHY RELATIONSHIPS contribute to emotional well-being and provide a support system for navigating life's challenges.

Steps for Cultivating Healthy Relationships:

1. COMMUNICATE OPENLY: Practice open and honest communication with friends, family, and partners. Share your thoughts and feelings and listen actively to others.

2. Set Boundaries: Establish and maintain healthy boundaries to protect your well-being and foster mutual respect in relationships.

3. Show Appreciation: Express gratitude and appreciation for the people in your life. Acknowledge their support and positive contributions.

4. Spend Quality Time: Invest time in building and maintaining meaningful connections. Engage in activities that strengthen your relationships and create positive experiences.

5. Address Conflicts: Address conflicts and misunderstandings promptly and constructively. Use effective conflict resolution techniques to maintain healthy relationships.

6. Pursuing Personal Growth:

PERSONAL GROWTH INVOLVES continuous learning and self-improvement. It enhances self-awareness, confidence, and overall well-being.

Steps for Pursuing Personal Growth:

1. SET PERSONAL GOALS: Set short-term and long-term personal goals that align with your values and aspirations. Goals provide direction and motivation for personal growth.

2. Engage in Learning: Continuously seek opportunities for learning and development. Read books, take courses, attend workshops, and seek new experiences.

3. Reflect and Evaluate: Regularly reflect on your progress and evaluate your experiences. Identify areas for improvement and celebrate your achievements.

4. Seek Feedback: Seek feedback from trusted individuals to gain new perspectives and insights. Use feedback to enhance your self-awareness and growth.

5. Embrace Change: Be open to change and new opportunities. Embrace challenges as opportunities for growth and learning.

Incorporating Mindfulness and Self-Care Practices

MINDFULNESS AND SELF-care practices are essential components of a healthy lifestyle. They promote emotional well-being, reduce stress, and enhance overall quality of life. Here are strategies for incorporating mindfulness and self-care into your daily routine:

1. Practicing Mindfulness:

MINDFULNESS INVOLVES being fully present in the moment and observing your thoughts, feelings, and sensations without judgment. It fosters self-awareness and emotional regulation.

Steps for Practicing Mindfulness:

1. MINDFUL BREATHING: Practice mindful breathing by focusing on your breath. Take slow, deep breaths and observe the sensation of air entering and leaving your body.

2. Body Scan: Perform a body scan by paying attention to different parts of your body, from your head to your toes. Notice any tension or discomfort and consciously relax those areas.

3. Mindful Observation: Observe your surroundings with full attention. Notice the details of your environment, such as colors, sounds, and textures, without judgment.

4. Mindful Eating: Practice mindful eating by savoring each bite of food. Pay attention to the taste, texture, and aroma of your food and eat slowly.

5. Meditation: Set aside time for meditation each day. Find a quiet place, sit comfortably, and focus on your breath or a specific meditation practice.

2. Engaging in Self-Care Activities:

SELF-CARE INVOLVES taking intentional actions to nurture your physical, mental, and emotional well-being. It is essential for maintaining a balanced lifestyle and preventing burnout.

Steps for Engaging in Self-Care Activities:

1. IDENTIFY SELF-CARE Needs: Reflect on your needs and identify activities that promote relaxation, joy, and well-being.

2. Schedule Self-Care: Schedule regular self-care activities into your daily or weekly routine. Treat self-care as a non-negotiable priority.

3. Engage in Hobbies: Pursue hobbies and activities that bring you joy and fulfillment. Whether it's reading, gardening, painting, or playing a musical instrument, make time for activities you enjoy.

4. Practice Relaxation: Incorporate relaxation techniques such as deep breathing, meditation, yoga, and aromatherapy into your routine.

5. Take Breaks: Take regular breaks throughout the day to rest and recharge. Short breaks can help prevent fatigue and improve focus.

3. Setting Healthy Boundaries:

HEALTHY BOUNDARIES are essential for protecting your time, energy, and well-being. They enable you to prioritize self-care and maintain healthy relationships.

Steps for Setting Healthy Boundaries:

1. IDENTIFY YOUR LIMITS: Reflect on your needs, values, and limits to identify your boundaries in different areas of your life.

2. Communicate Clearly: Clearly communicate your boundaries to others and explain their importance. Use assertive communication to express your needs.

3. Enforce Boundaries: Consistently enforce your boundaries and follow through with consequences if they are violated. Stand firm in your decisions.

4. Respect Others' Boundaries: Respect and honor the boundaries of others. Mutual respect is essential for maintaining healthy relationships.

5. Adjust as Needed: Regularly evaluate and adjust your boundaries as needed to reflect changes in your needs and circumstances.

4. Seeking Social Support:

SOCIAL SUPPORT IS CRUCIAL for emotional well-being. Building and maintaining a strong support network provides a sense of belonging, reduces stress, and enhances overall quality of life.

Steps for Seeking Social Support:

1. IDENTIFY SUPPORTIVE Individuals: Identify friends, family members, or colleagues who provide emotional support and understanding.

2. Communicate Openly: Share your thoughts, feelings, and experiences with supportive individuals. Open communication fosters connection and understanding.

3. Join Support Groups: Join support groups or online communities that align with your experiences and interests. These groups provide a sense of community and shared understanding.

4. Participate in Social Activities: Engage in social activities and events that allow you to connect with others and build meaningful relationships.

5. Offer Support: Offer emotional and practical support to others in your network. Reciprocity strengthens relationships and fosters a sense of mutual care.

5. Practicing Gratitude:

PRACTICING GRATITUDE involves regularly reflecting on and appreciating the positive aspects of your life. It fosters a positive mindset and enhances overall well-being.

Steps for Practicing Gratitude:

1. KEEP A GRATITUDE Journal: Keep a gratitude journal and write down three to five things you are grateful for each day. Reflect on the positive aspects of your life and the people who bring you joy.

2. Express Gratitude: Express gratitude to others by thanking them for their support, kindness, or positive contributions. Acknowledge and appreciate the people who make a difference in your life.

3. Practice Mindful Gratitude: Take moments throughout the day to practice mindful gratitude. Pause and reflect on the things you are thankful for, no matter how small.

4. Share Gratitude: Share your gratitude with others by discussing the positive aspects of your life and the things you appreciate. Sharing gratitude fosters a positive and supportive environment.

5. Celebrate Achievements: Celebrate your achievements and milestones, no matter how small. Recognize and appreciate your efforts and progress.

6. Engaging in Creative Expression:

CREATIVE EXPRESSION provides a healthy outlet for emotions and fosters a sense of fulfillment and joy. It enhances overall well-being and promotes self-discovery.

Steps for Engaging in Creative Expression:

1. IDENTIFY CREATIVE Interests: Identify creative activities that bring you joy and fulfillment, such as painting, drawing, writing, music, or crafting.

2. Set Aside Time: Set aside regular time for creative expression in your daily or weekly routine. Treat it as a priority and a source of joy.

3. Create a Space: Create a dedicated space for your creative activities. Ensure it is comfortable, organized, and conducive to creativity.

4. Experiment and Explore: Experiment with different forms of creative expression and explore new techniques and materials. Allow yourself to be playful and open to new experiences.

5. Share Your Work: Share your creative work with others, whether through social media, local events, or personal connections. Sharing your creativity fosters connection and validation.

7. Practicing Mindful Movement:

MINDFUL MOVEMENT INVOLVES integrating mindfulness into physical activities, such as yoga, tai chi, or mindful walking. It promotes physical health, emotional well-being, and self-awareness.

Steps for Practicing Mindful Movement:

1. CHOOSE AN ACTIVITY: Choose a physical activity that you enjoy and can practice mindfully, such as yoga, tai chi, or mindful walking.

2. Focus on the Present: Focus on the present moment and the sensations in your body as you move. Pay attention to your breath, posture, and the rhythm of your movements.

3. Practice Regularly: Incorporate mindful movement into your regular routine. Consistent practice enhances the benefits and fosters a sense of well-being.

4. Combine with Relaxation: Combine mindful movement with relaxation techniques, such as deep breathing or meditation, to enhance the overall experience.

5. Listen to Your Body: Listen to your body's signals and practice self-compassion. Modify movements as needed to ensure comfort and safety.

8. Seeking Professional Help:

SEEKING PROFESSIONAL help from therapists, counselors, or healthcare providers can provide valuable support and guidance for maintaining a healthy lifestyle.

Steps for Seeking Professional Help:

1. IDENTIFY YOUR NEEDS: Reflect on your needs and challenges to determine the type of professional help that would be beneficial.

2. Research Professionals: Research therapists, counselors, or healthcare providers who specialize in the areas you need support. Consider their qualifications, experience, and approach.

3. Schedule Consultations: Schedule consultations with potential professionals to discuss your needs and assess compatibility. Choose someone you feel comfortable with and trust.

4. Engage Actively: Engage actively in the therapeutic or healthcare process. Be open and honest about your experiences, challenges, and goals.

5. Follow Through: Follow through with recommended treatments, therapies, or practices. Consistency and commitment enhance the benefits of professional help.

Conclusion

Creating a healthy lifestyle involves integrating physical, mental, and emotional well-being into daily routines. By prioritizing physical health and wellness, developing a balanced lifestyle, and incorporating mindfulness and self-care practices, you can enhance your overall quality of life and build resilience against the challenges associated with growing up with a substance-abusing parent.

Remember that achieving a healthy lifestyle takes time, effort, and consistency. Be patient and compassionate with yourself as you navigate this journey. Seek support when needed, prioritize your well-being, and celebrate your progress and achievements. By taking these steps, you can move toward a life of health, balance, and fulfillment.

As you continue reading this book, you will find additional insights, strategies, and encouragement to support your healing journey. Each chapter provides practical tools and inspiring stories to help you navigate the complexities of your experiences and move toward a life of resilience and empowerment.

Chapter 14: Moving Forward: Setting Goals and Aspirations

Setting Realistic and Achievable Goals

Setting realistic and achievable goals is fundamental to personal growth and success. Goals provide direction, motivation, and a sense of purpose. For adult children of substance abusers, goal setting can be a powerful tool for overcoming past challenges and creating a fulfilling future.

1. Understanding the Importance of Goal Setting:

GOALS GIVE YOUR LIFE direction and help you focus on what's important. They provide a roadmap for personal and professional growth and help you measure progress and success.

2. Identifying Your Values and Priorities:

YOUR GOALS SHOULD ALIGN with your values and priorities. Reflect on what matters most to you and use these insights to guide your goal-setting process.

Steps for Identifying Values and Priorities:

1. REFLECT ON YOUR Values: Take time to reflect on your core values, such as integrity, compassion, creativity, and growth. Consider how these values influence your decisions and actions.

2. Assess Your Priorities: Identify your top priorities in different areas of your life, such as career, relationships, health, and personal development.

3. Align Goals with Values: Ensure that your goals align with your values and priorities. This alignment will provide motivation and a sense of fulfillment.

3. Setting SMART Goals:

SMART GOALS ARE SPECIFIC, measurable, achievable, relevant, and time-bound. This framework helps you create clear and actionable goals.

Steps for Setting SMART Goals:

1. SPECIFIC: DEFINE your goal clearly and specifically. Avoid vague or ambiguous language. For example, instead of saying "I want to be healthier," specify "I want to lose 10 pounds in the next three months by exercising regularly and eating a balanced diet."

2. Measurable: Ensure that your goal is measurable so you can track your progress. Identify specific criteria for success. For example, "I will exercise for 30 minutes, five days a week."

3. Achievable: Set realistic and achievable goals. Consider your current situation, resources, and constraints. Ensure that your goal is challenging but attainable.

4. Relevant: Ensure that your goal is relevant to your values, priorities, and long-term aspirations. It should contribute to your overall growth and fulfillment.

5. Time-Bound: Set a specific deadline for achieving your goal. This creates a sense of urgency and helps you stay focused and motivated.

4. Breaking Down Goals into Actionable Steps:

BREAKING DOWN YOUR goals into smaller, manageable steps makes them more achievable and less overwhelming. This approach also allows you to track progress and celebrate milestones along the way.

Steps for Breaking Down Goals:

1. IDENTIFY MAJOR MILESTONES: Break down your goal into major milestones or stages. These are significant achievements that bring you closer to your overall goal.

2. Create Actionable Steps: For each milestone, identify specific actions or tasks you need to complete. These should be clear and actionable.

3. Set Deadlines: Assign deadlines to each action step and milestone to create a timeline for achieving your goal.

4. Track Progress: Regularly track your progress and make adjustments as needed. Celebrate your achievements and learn from any setbacks.

5. Staying Motivated and Focused:

MAINTAINING MOTIVATION and focus is essential for achieving your goals. Here are strategies to stay on track:

Strategies for Staying Motivated:

1. VISUALIZE SUCCESS: Visualize the successful achievement of your goal and the positive impact it will have on your life. This can enhance motivation and commitment.

2. Seek Support: Share your goals with supportive friends, family members, or mentors. They can provide encouragement, accountability, and valuable feedback.

3. Stay Flexible: Be open to adjusting your goals and action steps as needed. Flexibility allows you to adapt to changing circumstances and stay on track.

4. Reward Yourself: Reward yourself for achieving milestones and completing action steps. This reinforces positive behavior and maintains motivation.

5. Reflect on Progress: Regularly reflect on your progress and the steps you've taken. Acknowledge your efforts and the growth you've experienced.

Overcoming Obstacles to Personal Growth

OBSTACLES ARE A NATURAL part of any growth journey. Recognizing and overcoming these obstacles is crucial for personal development and achieving your goals.

1. Identifying Common Obstacles:

UNDERSTANDING COMMON obstacles can help you anticipate and address them effectively. Here are some obstacles you may encounter:

Common Obstacles to Personal Growth:

1. FEAR OF FAILURE: Fear of failure can prevent you from taking risks and pursuing your goals. It can lead to procrastination and self-doubt.

2. Lack of Confidence: Low self-confidence can hinder your ability to take action and pursue opportunities. It can create a negative self-image and limit your potential.

3. Procrastination: Procrastination can delay progress and create unnecessary stress. It often stems from fear, overwhelm, or lack of motivation.

4. Negative Self-Talk: Negative self-talk can undermine your confidence and motivation. It involves self-criticism and doubt that can hinder your progress.

5. Limited Resources: Limited resources, such as time, money, or support, can create obstacles to achieving your goals. These constraints require creative problem-solving and resource management.

6. External Challenges: External challenges, such as health issues, family responsibilities, or work demands, can impact your ability to focus on your goals.

2. Developing Resilience and Growth Mindset:

RESILIENCE AND A GROWTH mindset are essential for overcoming obstacles and persisting through challenges. These qualities enable you to view setbacks as opportunities for growth and learning.

Steps for Developing Resilience and Growth Mindset:

1. EMBRACE CHALLENGES: View challenges as opportunities for growth and learning. Embrace them with a positive and proactive attitude.

2. Learn from Setbacks: Reflect on setbacks and identify the lessons they offer. Use these insights to improve and move forward.

3. Cultivate Self-Compassion: Practice self-compassion by treating yourself with kindness and understanding. Acknowledge your efforts and progress, even when things don't go as planned.

4. Stay Persistent: Stay persistent and committed to your goals, even when faced with obstacles. Persistence is key to achieving long-term success.

5. Seek Support: Reach out to supportive individuals for encouragement and guidance. Their support can provide valuable perspectives and motivation.

3. Managing Fear and Self-Doubt:

FEAR AND SELF-DOUBT can be significant barriers to personal growth. Managing these emotions involves building confidence and taking intentional actions to overcome them.

Steps for Managing Fear and Self-Doubt:

1. IDENTIFY FEARS: Identify the specific fears and doubts that are holding you back. Acknowledge their presence and understand their impact on your behavior.

2. Challenge Negative Thoughts: Challenge negative thoughts and replace them with positive and empowering beliefs. Use positive affirmations to reinforce a positive self-image.

3. Take Small Steps: Take small, incremental steps towards your goals. Gradual progress can build confidence and reduce fear.

4. Visualize Success: Visualize yourself successfully achieving your goals and overcoming obstacles. This can enhance motivation and reduce anxiety.

5. Celebrate Achievements: Celebrate your achievements, no matter how small. Acknowledge your progress and build on your successes.

4. Developing Effective Time Management:

Effective time management is crucial for balancing responsibilities and making progress towards your goals. It involves prioritizing tasks, setting boundaries, and staying organized.

Steps for Developing Effective Time Management:

1. SET PRIORITIES: Identify and prioritize tasks based on their importance and urgency. Focus on high-priority tasks that align with your goals.

2. Create a Schedule: Create a daily or weekly schedule that allocates time for specific tasks and activities. Include time for self-care and relaxation.

3. Set Boundaries: Set boundaries to protect your time and energy. Learn to say no to commitments that do not align with your priorities.

4. Avoid Distractions: Minimize distractions by creating a focused work environment and setting specific times for checking emails or social media.

5. Review and Adjust: Regularly review your schedule and make adjustments as needed. Flexibility allows you to adapt to changing circumstances and stay on track.

5. Seeking Professional Help and Mentorship:

PROFESSIONAL HELP AND mentorship can provide valuable guidance, support, and expertise. They can help you navigate obstacles and achieve your goals.

Steps for Seeking Professional Help and Mentorship:

1. IDENTIFY NEEDS: Identify the areas where you need support or guidance. This could include career development, personal growth, or specific skills.

2. Research Professionals: Research professionals or mentors who specialize in these areas. Consider their qualifications, experience, and approach.

3. Schedule Consultations: Schedule consultations to discuss your needs and assess compatibility. Choose someone you feel comfortable with and trust.

4. Engage Actively: Engage actively in the mentorship or professional relationship. Be open and honest about your experiences, challenges, and goals.

5. Follow Through: Follow through with recommended actions and practices. Consistency and commitment enhance the benefits of professional help and mentorship.

6. Leveraging Resources and Tools:

UTILIZING AVAILABLE resources and tools can enhance your ability to overcome obstacles and achieve your goals. These resources may include books, courses, apps, and online communities.

Steps for Leveraging Resources and Tools:

1. IDENTIFY RESOURCES: Identify resources that align with your goals and needs. This could include self-help books, online courses, productivity apps, or support groups.

2. Research Options: Research available options and consider their content, format, and reviews. Choose resources that provide practical and actionable guidance.

3. Engage and Apply: Engage with the chosen resources and apply the insights and practices to your life. Consistent application enhances the benefits.

4. Evaluate and Adjust: Regularly evaluate the effectiveness of the resources and make adjustments as needed. Seek out new resources to continue your growth.

Planning for a Fulfilling Future

PLANNING FOR A FULFILLING future involves setting long-term goals, creating a comprehensive plan, and taking intentional actions to achieve your aspirations. It requires a proactive and strategic approach to ensure that your future aligns with your values, priorities, and vision.

1. Creating a Vision for Your Future:

A CLEAR VISION FOR your future provides direction and motivation. It reflects your values, aspirations, and the life you want to create.

Steps for Creating a Vision for Your Future:

1. REFLECT ON YOUR Values: Reflect on your core values and how they influence your vision for the future. Consider what matters most to you in different areas of your life.

2. Visualize Your Ideal Life: Take time to visualize your ideal life. Imagine different aspects, such as career, relationships, health, personal growth, and leisure.

3. Write a Vision Statement: Write a vision statement that captures your aspirations and the life you want to create. This statement serves as a guiding star for your future.

4. Set Long-Term Goals: Based on your vision, set long-term goals that align with your aspirations. These goals provide a roadmap for achieving your vision.

5. Review and Adjust: Regularly review and adjust your vision and goals as needed to reflect changes in your values, priorities, or circumstances.

2. Developing a Comprehensive Plan:

A COMPREHENSIVE PLAN outlines the steps and strategies needed to achieve your long-term goals. It provides a structured approach to realizing your vision.

Steps for Developing a Comprehensive Plan:

1. BREAK DOWN GOALS: Break down your long-term goals into smaller, actionable steps. Identify the major milestones and tasks needed to achieve each goal.

2. Create a Timeline: Create a timeline that allocates specific timeframes for achieving each milestone and task. Ensure that the timeline is realistic and achievable.

3. Identify Resources: Identify the resources needed to achieve your goals, such as time, money, support, and tools. Plan how to acquire and utilize these resources.

4. Set Benchmarks: Set benchmarks to measure progress and ensure that you stay on track. Regularly review and assess your progress against these benchmarks.

5. Stay Flexible: Stay flexible and open to adjusting your plan as needed. Life is dynamic, and being adaptable allows you to navigate changes and stay focused on your goals.

3. Building a Support Network:

A STRONG SUPPORT NETWORK provides emotional, psychological, and practical support. It enhances your ability to achieve your goals and navigate challenges.

Steps for Building a Support Network:

1. IDENTIFY SUPPORTIVE Individuals: Identify friends, family members, mentors, or colleagues who provide encouragement, guidance, and support.

2. Communicate Your Goals: Share your goals and vision with supportive individuals. Their understanding and encouragement can enhance your motivation and commitment.

3. Seek Feedback: Seek feedback and advice from your support network. Their perspectives can provide valuable insights and help you refine your plans.

4. Offer Support: Offer support to others in your network. Reciprocity strengthens relationships and fosters a sense of mutual care.

5. Engage Regularly: Engage regularly with your support network. Maintain open communication and actively participate in building and maintaining these relationships.

4. Investing in Personal and Professional Development:

CONTINUOUS LEARNING and development are essential for achieving your goals and realizing your vision. Investing in personal and professional growth enhances your skills, knowledge, and potential.

Steps for Investing in Personal and Professional Development:

1. Identify Areas for Growth: Reflect on your strengths and areas for improvement. Identify the skills and knowledge needed to achieve your goals.

2. Seek Learning Opportunities: Seek out learning opportunities such as courses, workshops, books, and online resources. Choose those that align with your goals and interests.

3. Set Development Goals: Set specific goals for your personal and professional development. Create a plan to achieve these goals and track your progress.

4. Engage in Mentorship: Seek mentorship and guidance from experienced individuals. Their insights and support can enhance your growth and development.

5. Apply Learnings: Apply the knowledge and skills gained from learning opportunities to your personal and professional life. Continuous application enhances the benefits.

5. Fostering Work-Life Balance:

ACHIEVING A FULFILLING future involves balancing work, personal life, and self-care. A healthy work-life balance enhances well-being and overall quality of life.

Steps for Fostering Work-Life Balance:

1. SET BOUNDARIES: Set clear boundaries between work and personal life. Ensure that you allocate time for relaxation, hobbies, and relationships.

2. Prioritize Self-Care: Prioritize self-care by incorporating regular activities that promote relaxation, joy, and well-being into your routine.

3. Manage Time Effectively: Use effective time management strategies to balance work and personal responsibilities. Schedule time for self-care and leisure.

4. Seek Flexibility: Seek flexibility in your work arrangements, if possible. Flexible work options can enhance your ability to balance different aspects of your life.

5. Reflect and Adjust: Regularly reflect on your work-life balance and make adjustments as needed. Ensure that you maintain harmony between work and personal life.

6. Planning for Financial Security:

FINANCIAL SECURITY is a crucial component of a fulfilling future. Planning and managing your finances effectively ensures stability and freedom to pursue your aspirations.

Steps for Planning for Financial Security:

1. SET FINANCIAL GOALS: Set short-term and long-term financial goals that align with your vision for the future. These goals provide direction for your financial planning.

2. Create a Budget: Create a budget that outlines your income, expenses, and savings. Ensure that your budget supports your financial goals and priorities.

3. Save and Invest: Develop a savings and investment strategy to build wealth and achieve financial security. Consider retirement accounts, investment portfolios, and emergency funds.

4. Manage Debt: Develop a plan to manage and reduce debt. Focus on paying off high-interest debt and avoiding unnecessary new debt.

5. Seek Financial Advice: Seek advice from financial advisors or planners to develop a comprehensive financial plan. Their expertise can help you make informed decisions and optimize your financial strategy.

7. Embracing Change and Adaptability:

EMBRACING CHANGE AND adaptability are essential for navigating the dynamic nature of life. Being open to change allows you to seize new opportunities and overcome challenges.

Steps for Embracing Change and Adaptability:

1. STAY OPEN-MINDED: Stay open-minded and willing to explore new opportunities and experiences. Embrace change as a natural and positive aspect of life.

2. Develop Flexibility: Cultivate flexibility in your plans and goals. Be willing to adjust and adapt to changing circumstances and new information.

3. Build Resilience: Develop resilience by viewing challenges as opportunities for growth and learning. Stay persistent and proactive in pursuing your goals.

4. Seek New Experiences: Seek new experiences that push you out of your comfort zone. Embrace learning and growth opportunities that arise from change.

5. Reflect on Adaptability: Regularly reflect on your adaptability and growth. Acknowledge your ability to navigate change and the positive impact it has on your life.

8. Cultivating Gratitude and Positivity:

CULTIVATING GRATITUDE and a positive mindset enhances your overall well-being and outlook on life. It fosters a sense of contentment and fulfillment.

Steps for Cultivating Gratitude and Positivity:

1. PRACTICE GRATITUDE: Regularly reflect on and express gratitude for the positive aspects of your life. Keep a gratitude journal and acknowledge the people and experiences you appreciate.

2. Focus on Positives: Focus on the positive aspects of your experiences and challenges. Seek out the lessons and growth opportunities in difficult situations.

3. Surround Yourself with Positivity: Surround yourself with positive and supportive individuals. Engage in activities and environments that promote positivity and joy.

4. Celebrate Achievements: Celebrate your achievements and milestones, no matter how small. Acknowledge your progress and the positive impact of your efforts.

5. Maintain a Positive Mindset: Cultivate a positive mindset by practicing self-compassion, optimism, and resilience. Focus on your strengths and potential for growth.

Conclusion

Setting goals and aspirations is a powerful tool for personal growth and fulfillment. By setting realistic and achievable goals, overcoming obstacles, and planning for a fulfilling future, you can create a life that aligns with your values, priorities, and vision. Remember that achieving your goals takes time, effort, and resilience. Be patient and compassionate with yourself as you navigate this journey.

Seek support from your network, invest in continuous learning and development, and maintain a healthy work-life balance. Embrace change and adaptability, and cultivate gratitude and positivity to enhance your overall well-being. By taking these steps, you can move forward with confidence and create a future that brings you joy, fulfillment, and success.

As you continue reading this book, you will find additional insights, strategies, and encouragement to support your healing journey. Each chapter provides practical tools and inspiring stories to help you navigate the complexities of your experiences and move toward a life of resilience and empowerment.

Chapter 15: Inspiring Stories of Resilience

Introduction

Resilience is the ability to adapt and thrive despite facing adversity and challenges. For adult children of substance abusers, resilience often involves overcoming significant obstacles and transforming personal pain into strength and purpose. This chapter shares inspiring real-life stories of individuals who have overcome parental addiction, highlighting the lessons learned from their personal journeys. These stories serve as a testament to the human spirit's capacity for growth and recovery and offer encouragement and hope for readers facing similar challenges.

Real-Life Stories of Overcoming Parental Addiction

1. Emma's Journey: From Chaos to Clarity

EMMA GREW UP IN A HOUSEHOLD marked by her father's alcoholism. The instability and unpredictability of her home life left her feeling anxious and insecure. As the eldest of three siblings, Emma took on the role of caretaker, trying to shield her younger siblings from their father's erratic behavior and the chaos that ensued. Despite the challenges, Emma was determined to create a better life for herself and her family.

Challenges Faced:

- EMOTIONAL BURDEN: Emma constantly worried about her siblings and felt responsible for their well-being. This emotional burden affected her academic performance and social life.

- Lack of Support: With her mother working multiple jobs to make ends meet, Emma lacked emotional support and guidance from her parents.

- Financial Strain: The family's financial instability meant that Emma had to contribute to household expenses from a young age, limiting her opportunities for extracurricular activities and personal development.

Turning Point:

THE TURNING POINT FOR Emma came during her senior year of high school when a teacher noticed her potential and encouraged her to apply for college scholarships. With her teacher's support, Emma applied for and received several scholarships, enabling her to attend a university far from home.

Steps Taken:

1. SEEKING EDUCATION: Emma focused on her studies and embraced the opportunity to pursue higher education. She viewed education as a pathway to independence and a better future.

2. Building a Support Network: At university, Emma sought out mentors and supportive friends who provided guidance, encouragement, and a sense of belonging.

3. Therapy and Counseling: Emma sought therapy to address the emotional trauma of her childhood. Therapy helped her process her feelings, develop healthy coping mechanisms, and build self-esteem.

4. Setting Boundaries: Emma learned to set boundaries with her family, particularly her father, to protect her emotional well-being. She also encouraged her siblings to seek support and prioritize their own mental health.

***Outcome*:**

Emma graduated with honors and pursued a career in social work, dedicating her life to helping others who faced similar challenges. She maintained close relationships with her siblings and continued to support them emotionally and academically. Emma's journey from chaos to clarity exemplifies resilience and the transformative power of education, support, and self-care.

Lessons Learned:

- EDUCATION AS EMPOWERMENT: Pursuing education can provide opportunities for personal growth and independence.

- Importance of Support Networks: Building a support network of mentors, friends, and professionals can provide essential guidance and encouragement.

- Setting Boundaries: Establishing and maintaining boundaries is crucial for protecting emotional well-being and fostering healthy relationships.

2. James' Path to Emotional Resilience

JAMES GREW UP WITH a mother who struggled with prescription drug addiction. As a child, he often felt neglected and invisible, his emotional needs overshadowed by his mother's addiction. James coped by withdrawing emotionally and avoiding close relationships, fearing rejection and further emotional pain.

Challenges Faced:

- EMOTIONAL NEGLECT: James lacked the emotional support and validation needed for healthy development. His mother's addiction took precedence over his needs, leaving him feeling unworthy and unloved.

- Social Isolation: James's withdrawal from social interactions led to feelings of loneliness and isolation. He struggled to form meaningful connections and trust others.

- Internalized Shame: The stigma surrounding his mother's addiction caused James to internalize feelings of shame and self-blame, further impacting his self-esteem.

Turning Point:

THE TURNING POINT FOR James came in his thirties when his emotional detachment began to affect his marriage and his ability to connect with his children. At his wife's urging, James decided to seek therapy to address his unresolved childhood issues.

Steps Taken:

1. THERAPY AND COUNSELING: James found a therapist who specialized in attachment theory and trauma. Through therapy, he explored his childhood experiences and their impact on his adult behavior.

2. Joining Support Groups: James joined an Adult Children of Alcoholics (ACA) support group, where he connected with others who had similar experiences. The group provided a safe space for James to share his story and receive support.

3. Developing Emotional Awareness: James worked on developing emotional awareness and expressing his feelings. He practiced mindfulness and journaling to better understand and process his emotions.

4. Building Healthy Relationships: James focused on building healthy relationships with his family. He communicated openly with his wife and children, fostering trust and emotional intimacy.

Outcome:

With time and dedication, James opened up emotionally and built stronger connections with his family. He learned to express his feelings, set boundaries, and develop healthier relationship patterns. James's journey taught him the importance of emotional resilience and the power of community support. Today, he volunteers as a facilitator for his ACA group, helping others find their voice and path to healing.

Lessons Learned:

- THERAPY AS A HEALING Tool: Therapy can provide valuable insights and support for processing past trauma and developing emotional awareness.

- Value of Support Groups: Support groups offer a sense of community and shared understanding, reducing feelings of isolation.

- Importance of Emotional Expression: Developing emotional awareness and expressing feelings is essential for building healthy relationships and fostering personal growth.

3. Lily's Road to Self-Acceptance

LILY'S CHILDHOOD WAS marked by her mother's addiction to alcohol and her father's enabling behavior. Lily often felt responsible for her mother's well-being and struggled with feelings of guilt and shame. She developed perfectionistic tendencies, believing that if she were "perfect," she could somehow fix her family's problems.

Challenges Faced:

- PERFECTIONISM: LILY'S perfectionism led to high levels of stress and anxiety. She set unrealistic expectations for herself and felt constant pressure to excel in all areas of her life.

- Guilt and Shame: Lily internalized feelings of guilt and shame, believing that her mother's addiction was somehow her fault. These feelings impacted her self-esteem and self-worth.

- Lack of Self-Identity: Lily's focus on meeting others' expectations left her with a limited sense of self-identity. She struggled to understand her own needs, desires, and aspirations.

Turning Point:

IN HER LATE TWENTIES, Lily's perfectionism and anxiety became overwhelming. She realized that her coping mechanisms were no longer sustainable and decided to seek therapy.

Steps Taken:

1. THERAPY AND COUNSELING: Lily's therapist used a combination of humanistic therapy and mindfulness-based techniques. Together, they worked on addressing Lily's perfectionism, guilt, and self-criticism.

2. Practicing Self-Compassion: Lily practiced self-compassion by treating herself with kindness and understanding. She used positive affirmations to challenge negative self-beliefs and reinforce her self-worth.

3. Exploring Personal Interests: Lily explored her personal interests and passions, engaging in activities that brought her joy and fulfillment. She embraced creative expression through painting and writing.

4. Setting Boundaries: Lily set boundaries with her family to protect her emotional well-being. She communicated her needs clearly and prioritized self-care.

***Outcome*:**

Through therapy and self-compassion practices, Lily gradually let go of her need for perfection and embraced her authentic self. She learned to set boundaries, prioritize self-care, and practice self-acceptance. Lily's journey was transformative, allowing her to build a life rooted in self-love and authenticity. Today, Lily is a successful artist, using her creative talents to express her journey and inspire others.

Lessons Learned:

- SELF-COMPASSION AS Healing: Practicing self-compassion is essential for overcoming perfectionism and cultivating self-acceptance.

- Exploring Personal Interests: Engaging in activities that bring joy and fulfillment helps develop a sense of self-identity and purpose.

- Setting Boundaries: Establishing boundaries is crucial for protecting emotional well-being and fostering healthy relationships.

4. David's Quest for Inner Peace

DAVID GREW UP IN A volatile environment, with a father who was addicted to drugs and a mother who struggled with depression. The instability and chaos of his childhood left David with deep-seated anger and a tendency to lash out when feeling threatened or vulnerable.

Challenges Faced:

- ANGER AND AGGRESSION: David's unresolved anger manifested in aggressive behavior and difficulty managing his emotions. This impacted his relationships and career.

- Emotional Instability: The emotional instability of his childhood led to feelings of insecurity and vulnerability. David struggled to find inner peace and emotional balance.

- Self-Destructive Behaviors: David engaged in self-destructive behaviors, such as substance use and risky activities, as a way to cope with his emotional pain.

Turning Point:

IN HIS EARLY FORTIES, David's anger issues began to affect his career and personal relationships. Realizing the need for change, he decided to seek therapy to address his unresolved anger and trauma.

Steps Taken:

1. THERAPY AND COUNSELING: David's therapist specialized in anger management and trauma therapy. Through their sessions, David explored the root causes of his anger and developed healthier ways to express and manage his emotions.

2. Practicing Mindfulness: David incorporated mindfulness practices, such as meditation and deep breathing, into his daily routine. These practices helped him stay present and manage stress.

3. Joining Support Groups: David joined a support group for men dealing with anger issues. The group provided a safe space for David to share his experiences and learn from others.

4. Engaging in Positive Activities: David engaged in positive activities that promoted inner peace and emotional well-being, such as yoga, hiking, and creative writing.

Outcome:

With the support of therapy and the group, David experienced significant growth. He learned to recognize his anger triggers, communicate more effectively, and practice self-compassion. David's journey taught him the importance of inner peace and emotional regulation. Today, he works as a motivational speaker, sharing his story and helping others find their path to healing.

Lessons Learned:

- MINDFULNESS AS A TOOL: Mindfulness practices can help manage stress and promote emotional balance and inner peace.

- Value of Support Groups: Support groups offer a sense of community and shared understanding, reducing feelings of isolation.

- Positive Activities: Engaging in positive activities that promote well-being can help manage emotions and foster personal growth.

Lessons Learned from Personal Journeys

THE INSPIRING STORIES of Emma, James, Lily, and David highlight several key lessons that can guide others on their path to resilience and recovery. These lessons emphasize the importance of self-awareness, support, and proactive strategies for overcoming adversity.

1. Embrace Self-Awareness and Personal Growth:

SELF-AWARENESS IS THE foundation of personal growth. Understanding your thoughts, feelings, and behaviors enables you to make informed choices and take intentional actions toward healing and growth.

Key Points:

- REFLECT ON YOUR EXPERIENCES and their impact on your behavior and emotions.

- Seek therapy or counseling to gain insights and develop self-awareness.

- Practice mindfulness and self-reflection to stay connected to your inner self.

2. Seek and Cultivate Supportive Relationships:

SUPPORTIVE RELATIONSHIPS provide essential emotional and practical support. Building a strong support network can enhance your resilience and provide a sense of belonging.

Key Points:

- IDENTIFY SUPPORTIVE individuals in your life and communicate openly with them.

- Join support groups to connect with others who share similar experiences.

- Build relationships with mentors and professionals who can offer guidance and encouragement.

3. Practice Self-Compassion and Self-Care:

SELF-COMPASSION INVOLVES treating yourself with kindness and understanding. Prioritizing self-care ensures that you meet your physical, emotional, and mental needs.

Key Points:

- USE POSITIVE AFFIRMATIONS to challenge negative self-beliefs and reinforce self-worth.

- Engage in activities that bring you joy and fulfillment.

- Set boundaries to protect your emotional well-being and prioritize self-care.

4. Develop Healthy Coping Mechanisms:

HEALTHY COPING MECHANISMS help you manage stress, emotions, and challenges effectively. They promote resilience and emotional stability.

Key Points:

- PRACTICE MINDFULNESS and relaxation techniques to manage stress.

- Develop healthy outlets for emotions, such as exercise, creative expression, or journaling.

- Avoid self-destructive behaviors and seek positive ways to cope with difficulties.

5. Pursue Personal and Professional Development:

CONTINUOUS LEARNING and development enhance your skills, knowledge, and potential. Investing in personal and professional growth contributes to a fulfilling and successful life.

Key Points:

- SET PERSONAL AND PROFESSIONAL goals that align with your values and aspirations.

- Seek learning opportunities, such as courses, workshops, and mentorship.

- Apply the knowledge and skills gained to achieve your goals and create a meaningful life.

Encouragement and Hope for Readers

THE STORIES AND LESSONS shared in this chapter demonstrate that resilience and recovery are possible, regardless of the challenges faced. For readers who are adult children of substance abusers, these stories offer hope and inspiration. Here are key messages of encouragement:

1. You Are Not Alone:

MANY INDIVIDUALS HAVE faced similar challenges and have found ways to overcome them. You are not alone in your journey, and there is a community of support available to you.

2. Healing is Possible:

HEALING FROM THE TRAUMA of parental addiction is possible. With the right support, strategies, and mindset, you can create a life of resilience, growth, and fulfillment.

3. Take Small Steps:

PROGRESS OFTEN COMES from taking small, consistent steps toward your goals. Celebrate each achievement, no matter how small, and use it as motivation to continue moving forward.

4. Seek Support:

DON'T HESITATE TO SEEK support from friends, family, therapists, and support groups. Their encouragement and guidance can make a significant difference in your journey.

5. Embrace Your Strengths:

RECOGNIZE AND EMBRACE your strengths and the unique qualities that make you who you are. Use these strengths to overcome challenges and achieve your aspirations.

6. Be Kind to Yourself:

PRACTICE SELF-COMPASSION and be kind to yourself. Acknowledge your efforts and progress, and treat yourself with the same kindness and understanding that you would offer to a friend.

7. Focus on Your Future:

FOCUS ON CREATING A future that aligns with your values and aspirations. Set goals, develop a plan, and take intentional actions to build the life you envision.

Conclusion

The stories of resilience shared in this chapter highlight the power of the human spirit to overcome adversity and create a fulfilling life. Through self-awareness, support, self-compassion, healthy coping mechanisms, and personal growth, it is possible to transform the challenges of growing up with a substance-abusing parent into a source of strength and empowerment.

As you continue your journey, remember that resilience is a process, not a destination. Each step you take toward healing and growth is a testament to your strength and determination. Keep moving forward, seek support, and embrace the opportunities for growth and fulfillment that lie ahead. Your journey is unique, and your story of resilience can inspire others facing similar challenges.

This book has provided practical tools, inspiring stories, and encouragement to support your healing journey. As you navigate the complexities of your experiences, know that you have the power to create a life of resilience, empowerment, and joy.

Conclusion: Embracing Your Journey

Recap of Key Lessons

As we conclude this journey through the complexities and triumphs of life as an adult child of substance abusers, it's essential to reflect on the key lessons we've explored. Each chapter of this book has provided insights, strategies, and encouragement to help you navigate your path toward healing and empowerment. Here, we'll recap these vital lessons to reinforce their importance and utility in your ongoing journey.

1. Understanding Parental Addiction:

IN THE EARLY CHAPTERS, we delved into understanding substance abuse and its profound impact on family dynamics. Recognizing the nature of addiction and its ripple effects is crucial for contextualizing your experiences and initiating the healing process.

Key Points:

- ADDICTION IS A COMPLEX, chronic disease that affects the brain and behavior.

- Families of substance abusers often experience emotional turmoil, instability, and strained relationships.

- Understanding addiction helps in developing empathy and reducing self-blame.

2. The Emotional Roller Coaster:

NAVIGATING THE EMOTIONAL aftermath of growing up with a substance-abusing parent involves recognizing and processing complex feelings such as anger, guilt, and shame.

Key Points:

- IDENTIFYING AND ACKNOWLEDGING your emotions is the first step toward healing.

- Strategies like journaling, therapy, and support groups can help process these feelings.

- Emotional regulation techniques, such as mindfulness and deep breathing, are essential for managing intense emotions.

3. Coping Mechanisms: Healthy vs. Unhealthy:

UNDERSTANDING THE DIFFERENCE between healthy and unhealthy coping mechanisms is crucial for building resilience and avoiding further harm.

Key Points:

- UNHEALTHY COPING STRATEGIES, such as substance use or denial, can perpetuate the cycle of pain.

- Developing healthy coping skills, like exercise, creative expression, and seeking support, promotes well-being.

- Building resilience involves cultivating positive habits and learning from setbacks.

4. The Legacy of Trust Issues:

GROWING UP WITH A SUBSTANCE-abusing parent often leads to trust issues, which can affect your relationships and self-perception.

Key Points:

- TRUST ISSUES STEM from experiences of betrayal and inconsistency.

- Overcoming mistrust involves setting boundaries, practicing open communication, and engaging in trust-building activities.

- Healthy relationships are built on mutual respect, honesty, and emotional safety.

5. Navigating Family Dynamics:

MANAGING RELATIONSHIPS within a family affected by addiction is complex but essential for your mental and emotional health.

Key Points:

- ESTABLISHING AND MAINTAINING boundaries with addicted parents and siblings is crucial.

- Sibling dynamics can be complicated; open communication and mutual support are key.

- It's important to balance familial obligations with self-care and personal boundaries.

6. Healing the Inner Child:

HEALING THE INNER CHILD involves nurturing the parts of yourself that were hurt or neglected during childhood.

Key Points:

- UNDERSTANDING AND connecting with your inner child can help heal past wounds.

- Techniques such as guided imagery, play therapy, and creative expression are effective for inner child work.

- Self-compassion and self-love are foundational for healing and personal growth.

7. Developing Self-Worth and Identity:

REDISCOVERING AND AFFIRMING your self-worth and identity outside of familial roles is a pivotal step in your journey.

Key Points:

- SELF-WORTH IS INHERENT and independent of external validation.

- Exploring personal interests and passions helps build a strong sense of identity.

- Positive self-talk and affirmations can reinforce a healthy self-image.

8. Communication Skills for Conflict Resolution:

EFFECTIVE COMMUNICATION is vital for resolving conflicts and building healthy relationships.

Key Points:

- ACTIVE LISTENING, "I" statements, and nonverbal communication enhance understanding and reduce conflicts.

- Dealing with difficult conversations involves preparation, emotional regulation, and a focus on mutual respect.

- Conflict resolution within the family requires addressing underlying issues, creating a safe environment, and practicing forgiveness.

9. The Role of Therapy and Support Groups:

PROFESSIONAL HELP AND support groups play a crucial role in the healing process.

Key Points:

- THERAPY PROVIDES A safe, nonjudgmental space for self-exploration and healing.

- Support groups offer a sense of community and shared understanding.

- Finding the right therapist or support group involves identifying your needs, researching options, and building a comprehensive support network.

10. Overcoming Codependency:

BREAKING FREE FROM codependency involves recognizing unhealthy behaviors and developing independence and healthy interdependence.

Key Points:

- CODEPENDENCY OFTEN involves excessive emotional reliance and enabling behaviors.

- Overcoming codependency requires self-awareness, boundary-setting, and building self-esteem.

- Healthy relationships are based on mutual support, respect, and independence.

11. Establishing Financial Independence:

ACHIEVING FINANCIAL independence is crucial for personal empowerment and stability.

Key Points:

- FINANCIAL CHALLENGES faced by adult children of substance abusers include financial instability, lack of financial education, and emotional spending.

- Strategies for financial stability include budgeting, saving, investing, and managing debt.

- Planning for a secure financial future involves setting financial goals, creating a comprehensive financial plan, and seeking professional advice.

12. Building a Support Network:

A STRONG SUPPORT NETWORK is essential for emotional, psychological, and practical support.

Key Points:

- SUPPORTIVE RELATIONSHIPS provide validation, encouragement, and resilience.

- Building a support network involves identifying potential supporters, building trust, and nurturing relationships.

- Leveraging community resources, such as social services, support groups, and educational programs, enhances support and well-being.

13. Creating a Healthy Lifestyle:

A HEALTHY LIFESTYLE integrates physical, mental, and emotional well-being into daily routines.

Key Points:

- PHYSICAL HEALTH AND wellness are fundamental to overall well-being.

- Developing a balanced lifestyle involves regular physical activity, a balanced diet, adequate sleep, stress management, and cultivating healthy relationships.

- Incorporating mindfulness and self-care practices promotes emotional stability and resilience.

14. Moving Forward: Setting Goals and Aspirations:

SETTING REALISTIC AND achievable goals provides direction, motivation, and a sense of purpose.

Key Points:

- SETTING SMART GOALS (specific, measurable, achievable, relevant, time-bound) ensures clarity and actionability.

- Overcoming obstacles to personal growth involves developing resilience, managing fear and self-doubt, and seeking professional help.

- Planning for a fulfilling future requires creating a vision, developing a comprehensive plan, and investing in personal and professional development.

Embracing a Resilient and Empowered Future

AS YOU REFLECT ON THESE key lessons, it's time to embrace your journey and move forward with resilience and empowerment. Embracing your journey involves acknowledging your past, celebrating your strengths, and taking proactive steps toward a fulfilling future. Here's how to embrace a resilient and empowered future:

1. Acknowledge and Accept Your Past:

YOUR PAST EXPERIENCES have shaped you, but they do not define you. Acknowledge your past, including the pain and challenges, and accept it as part of your journey.

Key Points:

- ACCEPTANCE INVOLVES recognizing your experiences without judgment or denial.

- Reflect on the lessons learned from your past and how they have contributed to your growth.

- Embrace your resilience and strength in overcoming adversity.

2. Celebrate Your Strengths and Achievements:

TAKE TIME TO CELEBRATE your strengths and achievements. Recognize the progress you have made and the effort you have invested in your healing and growth.

Key Points:

- REFLECT ON YOUR ACCOMPLISHMENTS, both big and small, and celebrate them.
- Acknowledge your strengths, such as resilience, empathy, and determination.
- Use your achievements as motivation to continue moving forward.

3. Set Intentions for Your Future:

SET CLEAR INTENTIONS for your future that align with your values, aspirations, and vision. Intentions provide a sense of purpose and direction for your journey.

Key Points:

- DEFINE YOUR INTENTIONS based on your values and what matters most to you.
- Write down your intentions and review them regularly to stay focused and motivated.
- Use your intentions as a guide for setting goals and making decisions.

4. Take Proactive Steps Toward Your Goals:

TAKE INTENTIONAL ACTIONS toward your goals and aspirations. Break down your goals into manageable steps and stay committed to your progress.

Key Points:

- CREATE A PLAN FOR achieving your goals, including actionable steps and timelines.

- Stay flexible and open to adjusting your plan as needed.

- Track your progress and celebrate milestones along the way.

5. Cultivate a Positive and Growth-Oriented Mindset:

A POSITIVE AND GROWTH-oriented mindset is essential for resilience and empowerment. Embrace challenges as opportunities for growth and stay focused on your potential.

Key Points:

- PRACTICE POSITIVE self-talk and affirmations to reinforce a healthy self-image.

- Embrace a growth mindset by viewing setbacks as learning opportunities.

- Surround yourself with positive influences and supportive individuals.

6. Prioritize Self-Care and Well-Being:

PRIORITIZE SELF-CARE and well-being in all aspects of your life. Taking care of yourself is crucial for maintaining resilience and achieving your goals.

Key Points:

- INCORPORATE SELF-CARE practices into your daily routine, such as exercise, relaxation, and hobbies.

- Set boundaries to protect your time and energy.

- Seek support from friends, family, and professionals when needed.

7. Embrace Change and Adaptability:

EMBRACE CHANGE AND adaptability as natural parts of life. Being open to change allows you to seize new opportunities and navigate challenges effectively.

Key Points:

- STAY OPEN-MINDED AND willing to explore new experiences.

- Cultivate flexibility in your plans and goals to adapt to changing circumstances.

- Reflect on your ability to navigate change and the positive impact it has on your growth.

Final Words of Encouragement and Support

AS WE CONCLUDE THIS journey together, I want to leave you with words of encouragement and support. Your path to healing and empowerment is unique, and your resilience and strength are remarkable. Here are some final thoughts to inspire and motivate you:

1. Believe in Yourself:

BELIEVE IN YOUR ABILITY to overcome challenges and create a fulfilling life. Trust in your strengths, potential, and resilience. You have already demonstrated incredible courage and determination in your journey.

2. Stay Committed to Your Growth:

STAY COMMITTED TO YOUR personal growth and well-being. Continue to invest in yourself, seek new opportunities for learning and development, and prioritize self-care. Your commitment to growth will lead to lasting positive change.

3. Seek and Cultivate Support:

SURROUND YOURSELF WITH supportive and understanding individuals who encourage and uplift you. Build and maintain a strong support network that provides emotional, psychological, and practical support.

4. Embrace Your Journey:

EMBRACE YOUR JOURNEY with compassion and gratitude. Acknowledge the progress you have made, celebrate your achievements, and view challenges as opportunities for growth. Your journey is a testament to your strength and resilience.

5. Keep Moving Forward:

KEEP MOVING FORWARD, no matter the obstacles you face. Take small, consistent steps toward your goals and stay focused on your vision for the future. Your persistence and determination will lead to success.

6. Practice Gratitude and Positivity:

CULTIVATE GRATITUDE and a positive mindset. Reflect on the positive aspects of your life, express gratitude for the support you receive, and maintain an optimistic outlook. Positivity and gratitude enhance well-being and resilience.

7. Inspire Others:

YOUR JOURNEY AND EXPERIENCES have the power to inspire and uplift others. Share your story, offer support, and be a beacon of hope for those facing similar challenges. Your resilience can make a meaningful difference in the lives of others.

Conclusion

As you embrace your journey and move forward with resilience and empowerment, remember that you are not alone. You have the strength, potential, and support needed to create a fulfilling and joyful life. This book has provided practical tools, inspiring stories, and encouragement to support your healing journey. Each step you take toward healing and growth is a testament to your courage and determination.

Keep believing in yourself, stay committed to your growth, and embrace your journey with compassion and gratitude. Your path to resilience and empowerment is a remarkable testament to the human spirit's capacity for transformation and renewal. You have the power to create a future that aligns with your values, aspirations, and vision. Embrace your journey, celebrate your progress, and continue moving forward with confidence and hope.

Don't miss out!

Visit the website below and you can sign up to receive emails whenever Timothy Scott Phillips publishes a new book. There's no charge and no obligation.

https://books2read.com/r/B-A-KCQWC-SQBJF

BOOKS 2 READ

Connecting independent readers to independent writers.

About the Author

Timothy Scott Phillips is a dedicated author specializing in non-fiction self-help books that empower readers to overcome challenges and embrace personal growth. With a passion for mental health, resilience, and self-improvement, Timothy combines research-based insights with practical strategies to inspire lasting change. His work reflects a deep commitment to helping individuals navigate life's complexities, build confidence, and unlock their full potential. When he's not writing, Timothy enjoys mentoring, exploring nature, and connecting with his readers to share stories of transformation and hope. His books are a testament to the power of perseverance and the human spirit.

www.ingramcontent.com/pod-product-compliance
Lightning Source LLC
LaVergne TN
LVHW041213150826
845673LV00001B/379